# PNA Photography Magazine

VOLUME 1 SUMMER/FALL  2017

PHOTO ART

Photography
Natacha Allard

Art's is a road towards a state of mind,
than everyone love contemplating!

Sometimes we look for canvases or pictures to decorate our house. Whatever room we want to embellish, we want something different.
Finding a canvas or picture that could make our happiness for a room is certainly not easy. Here is a photo book simple, colorful, modern and classic works of art that could please everyone!

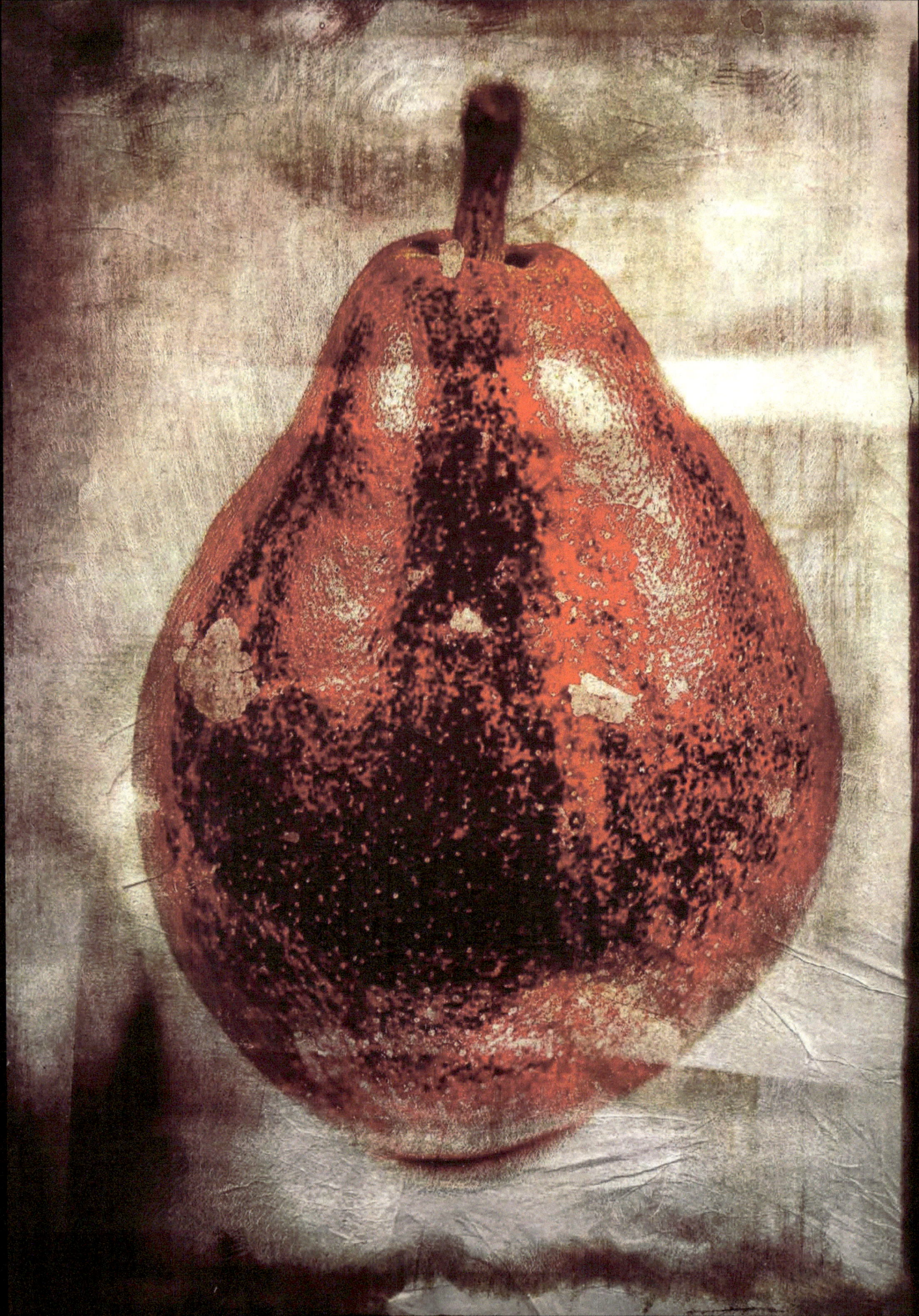

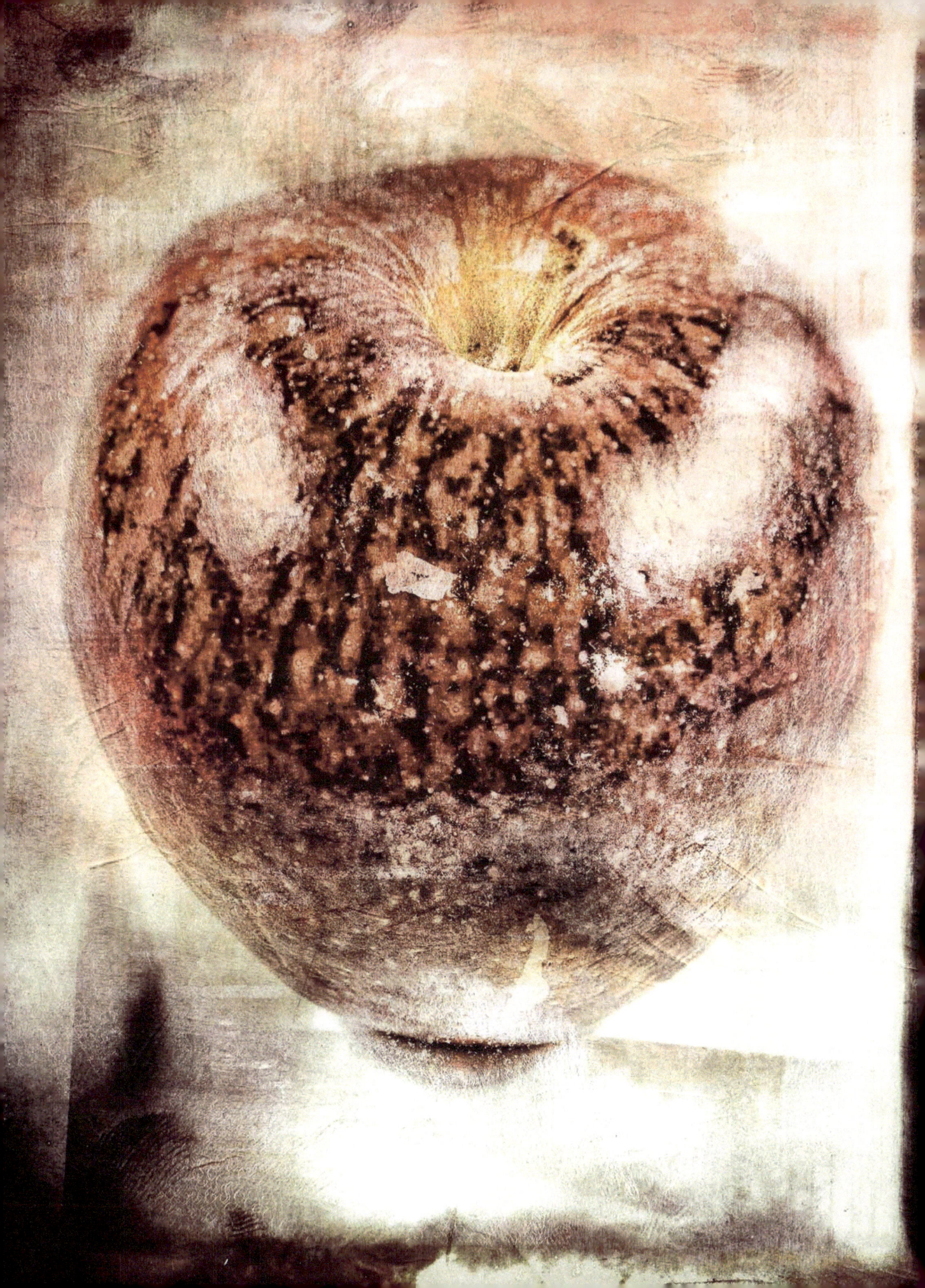

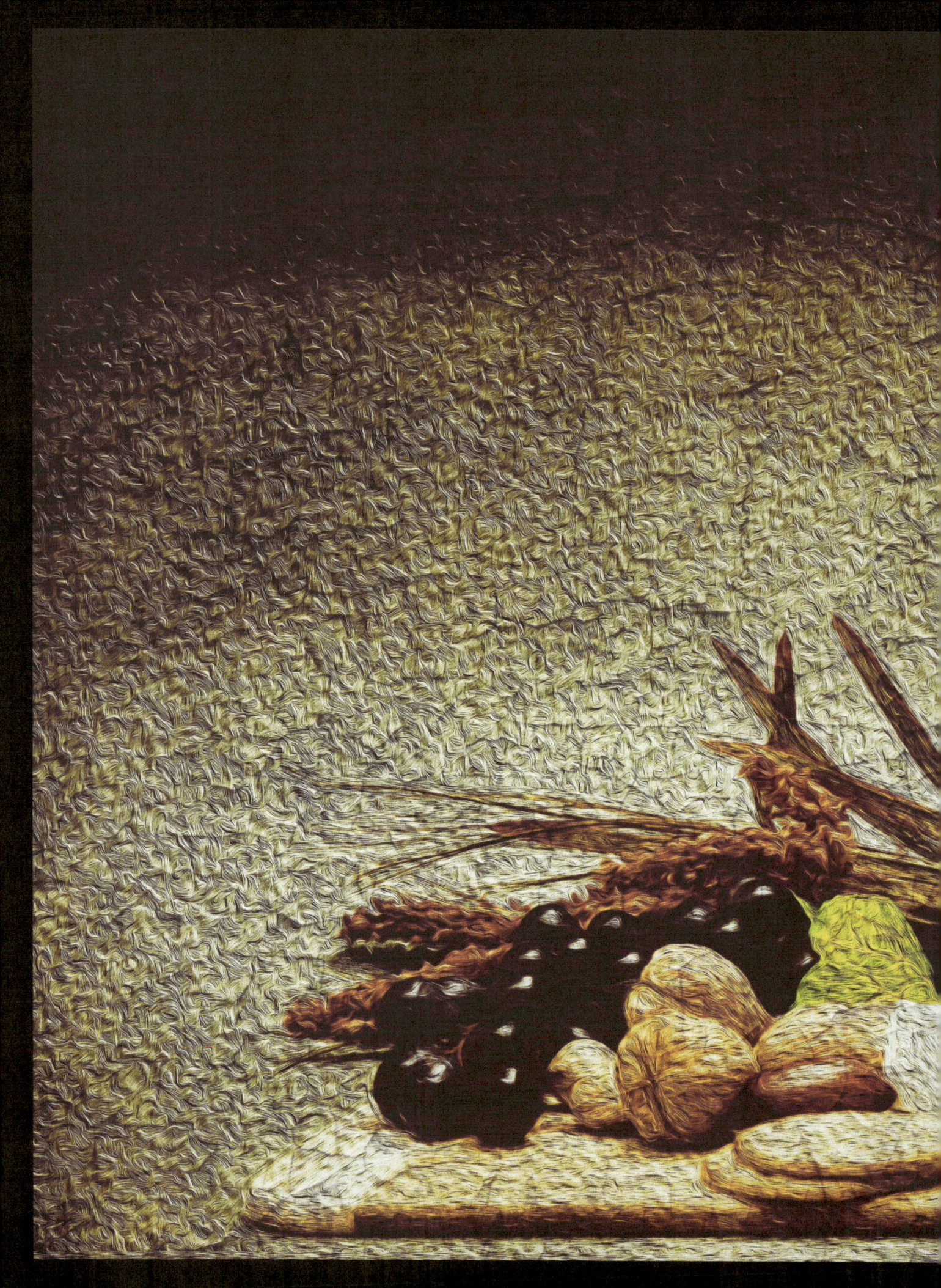

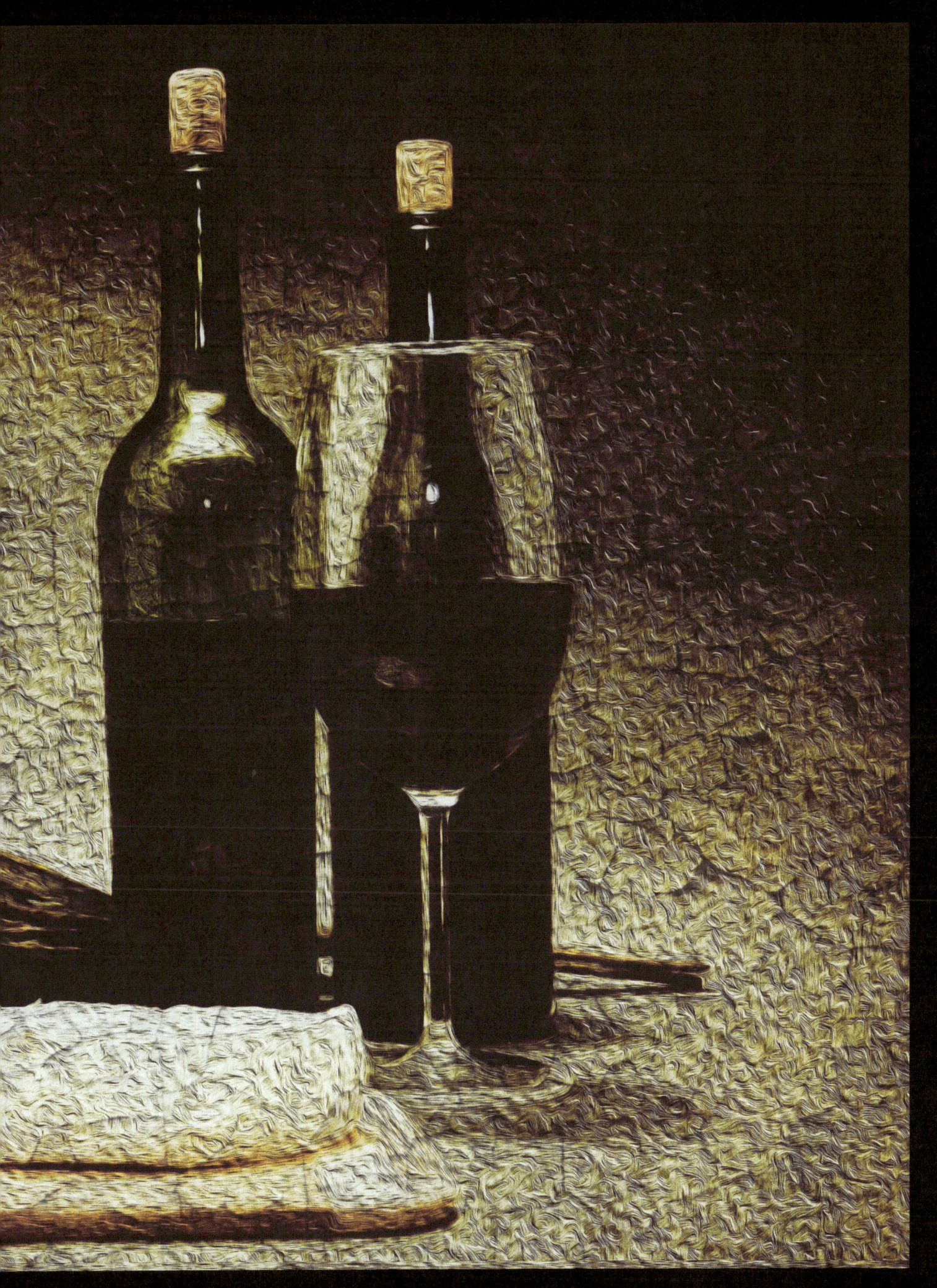

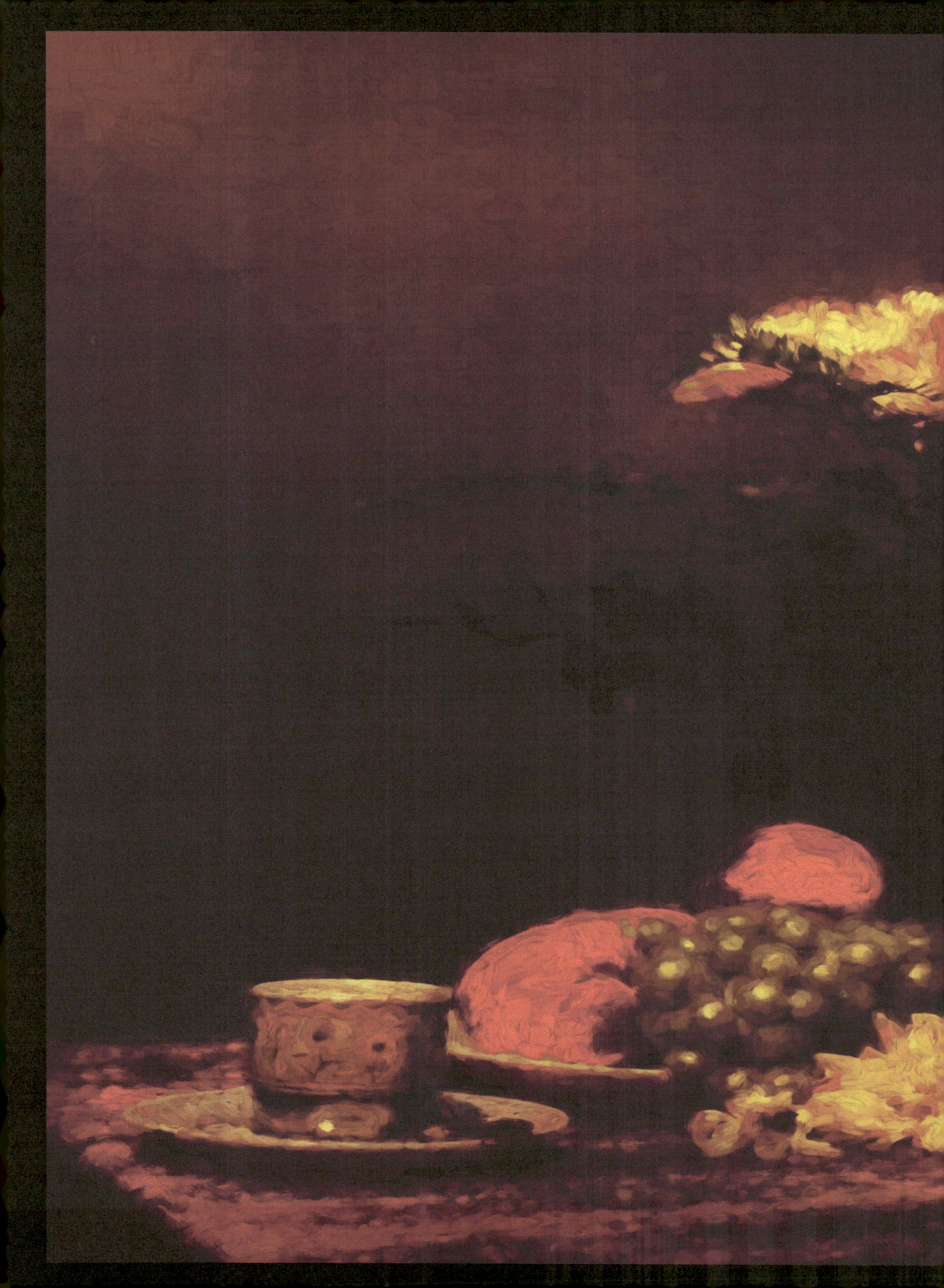

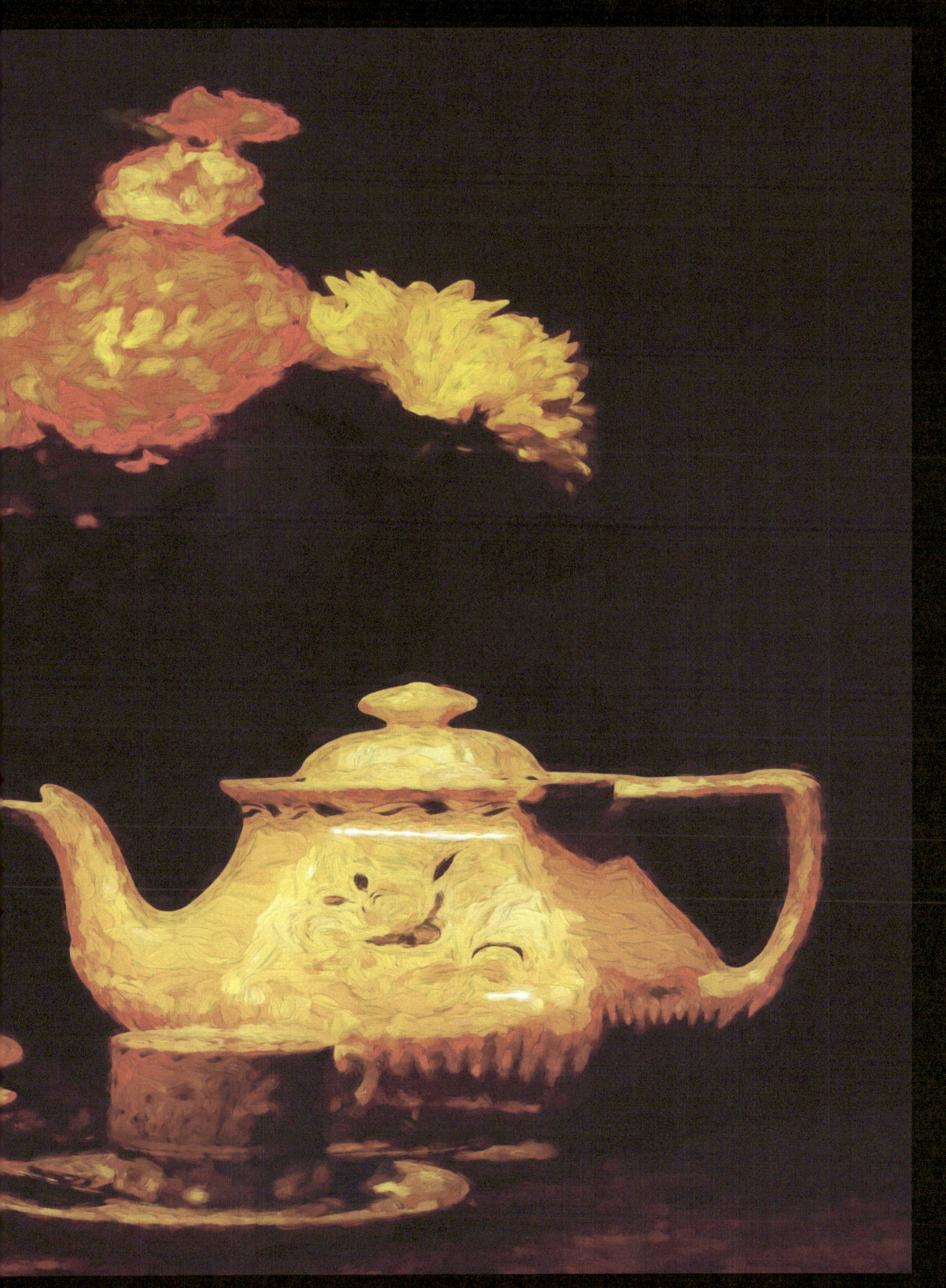

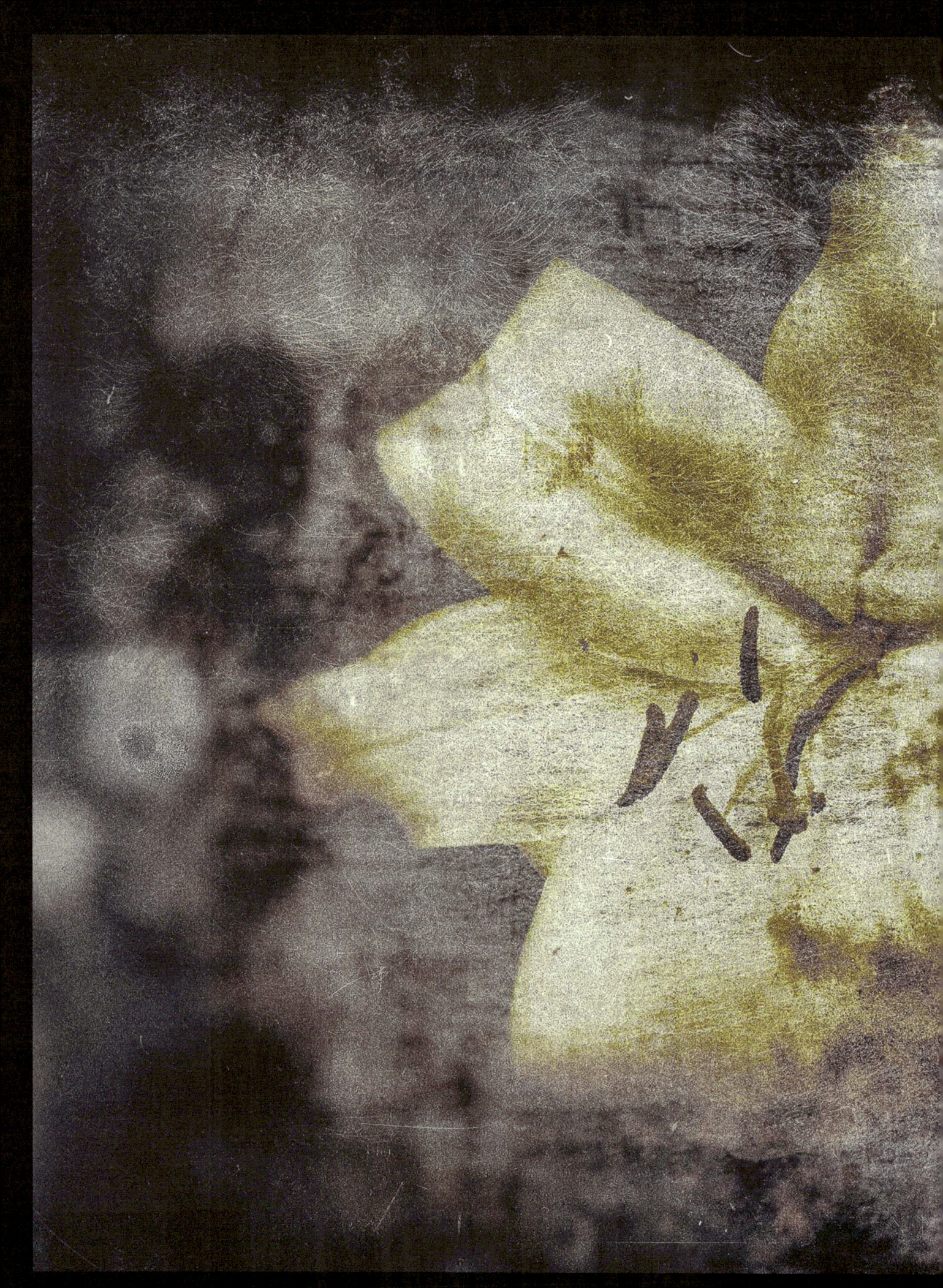

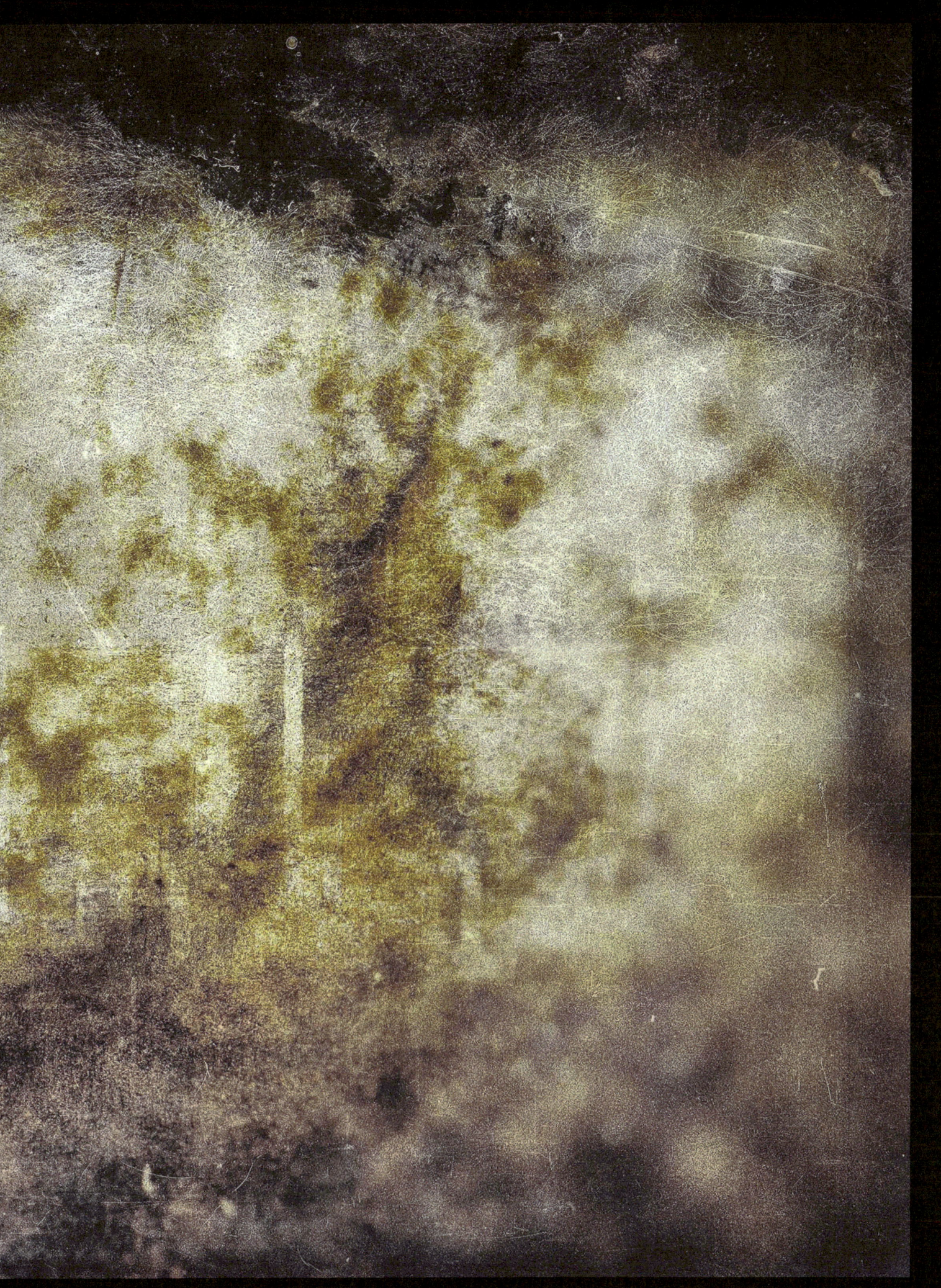

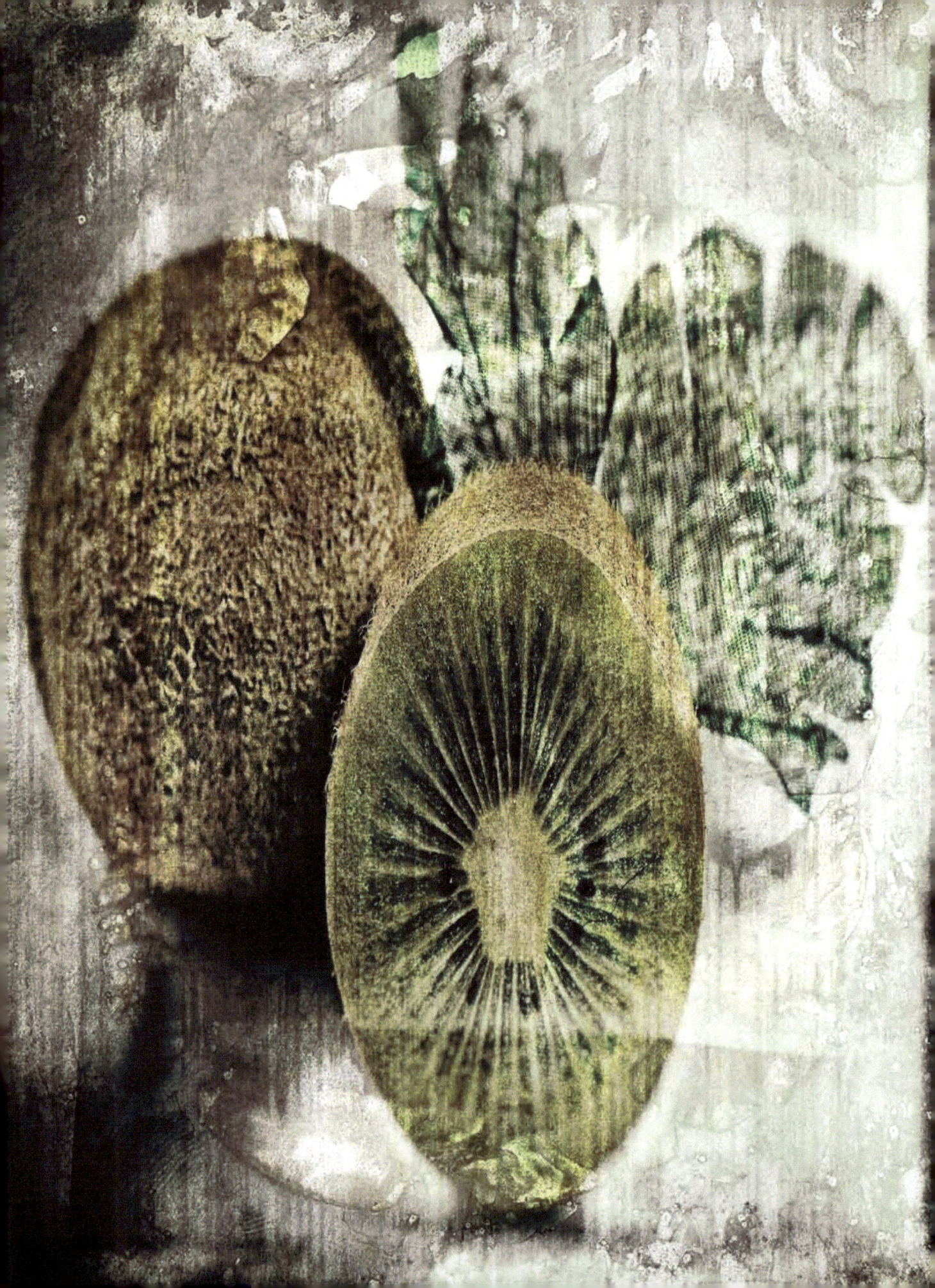

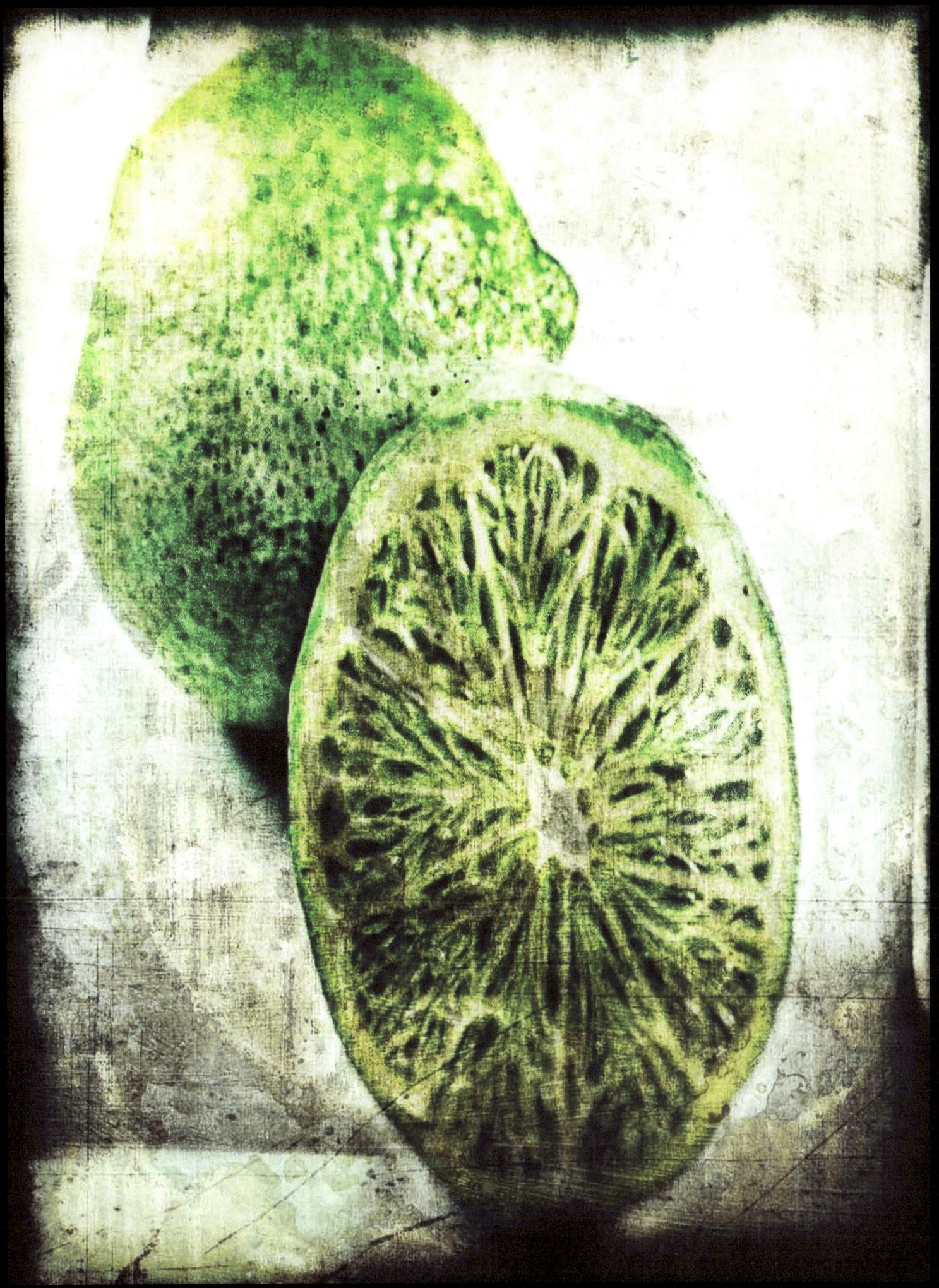

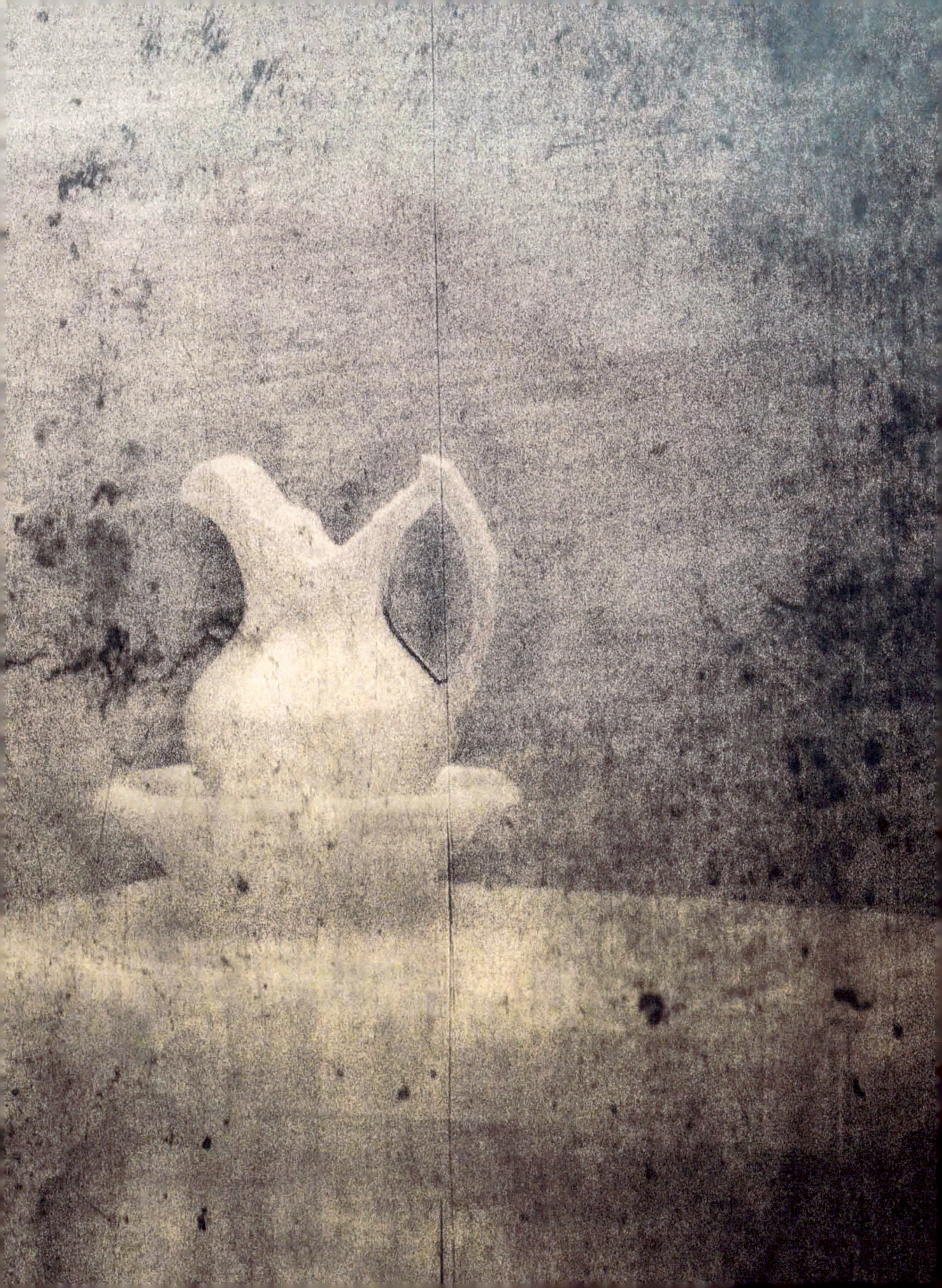

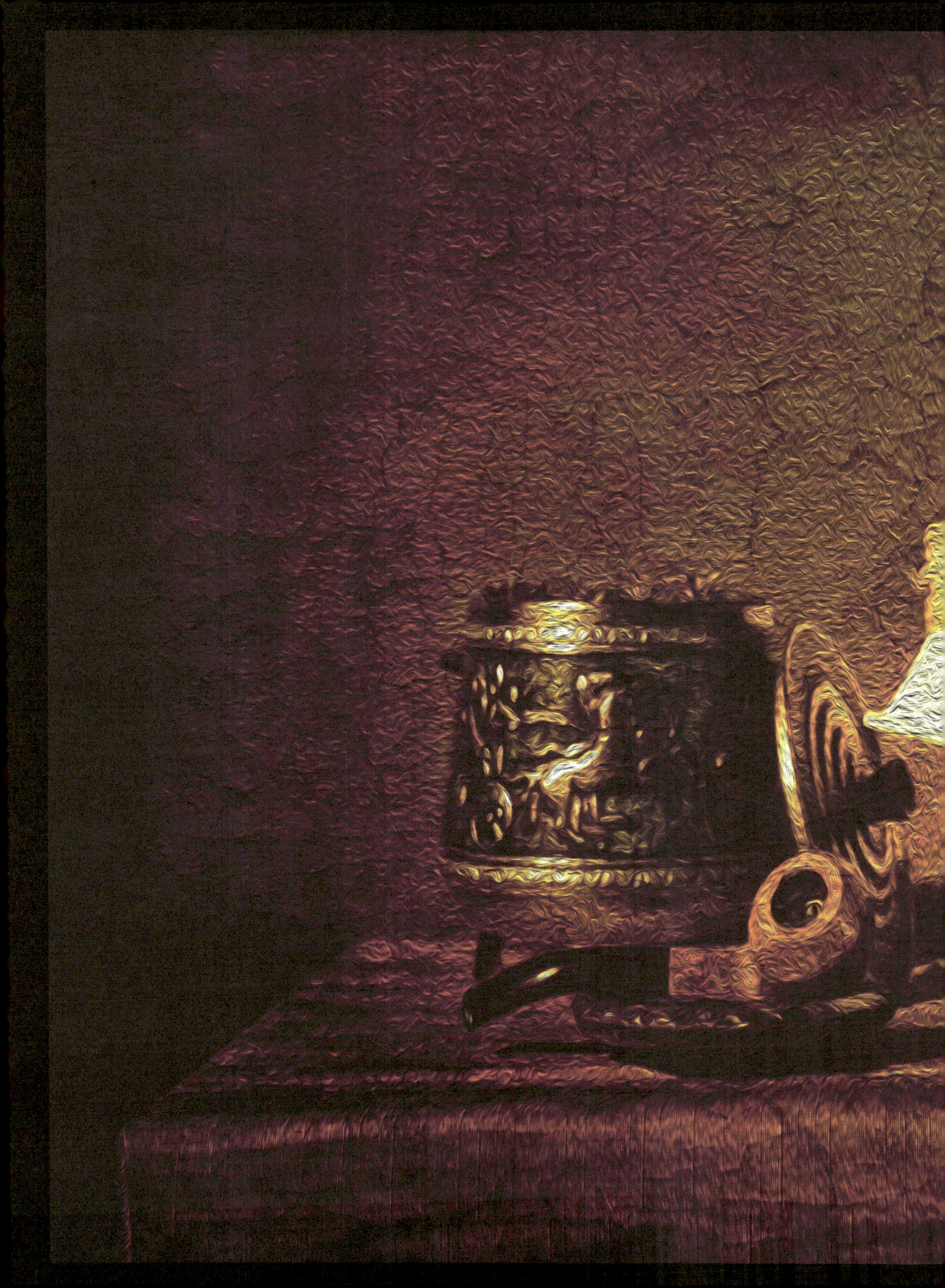

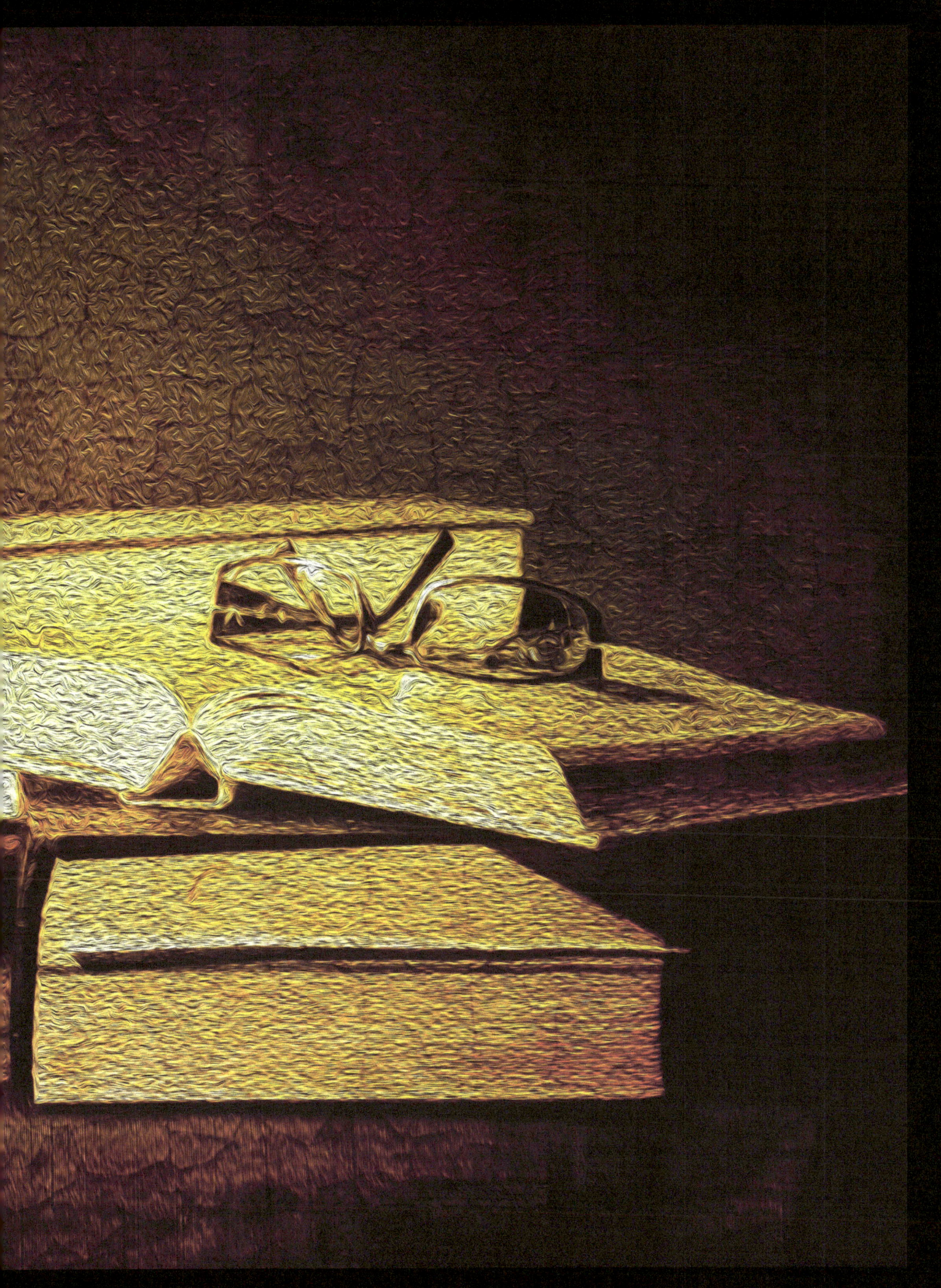

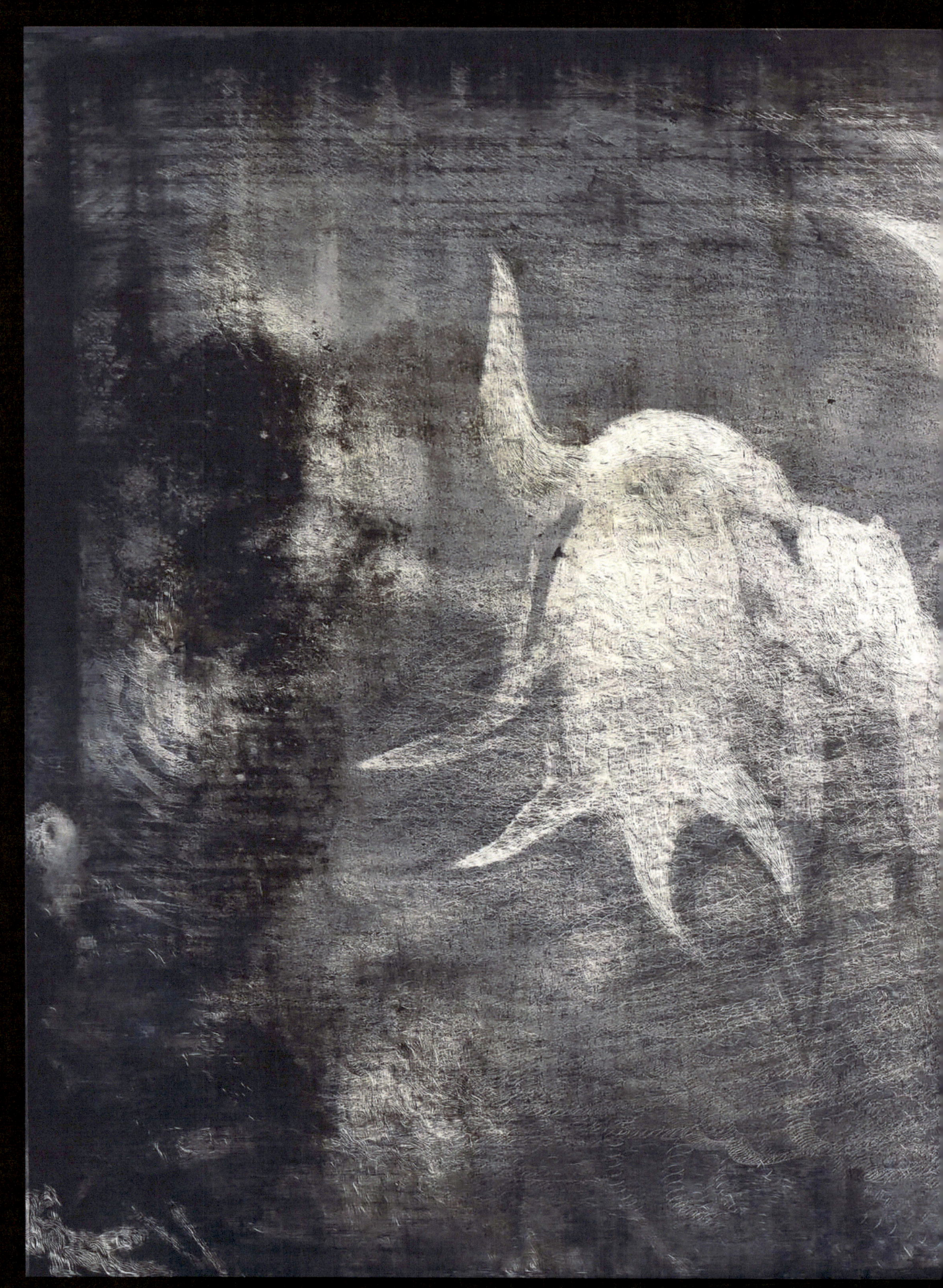

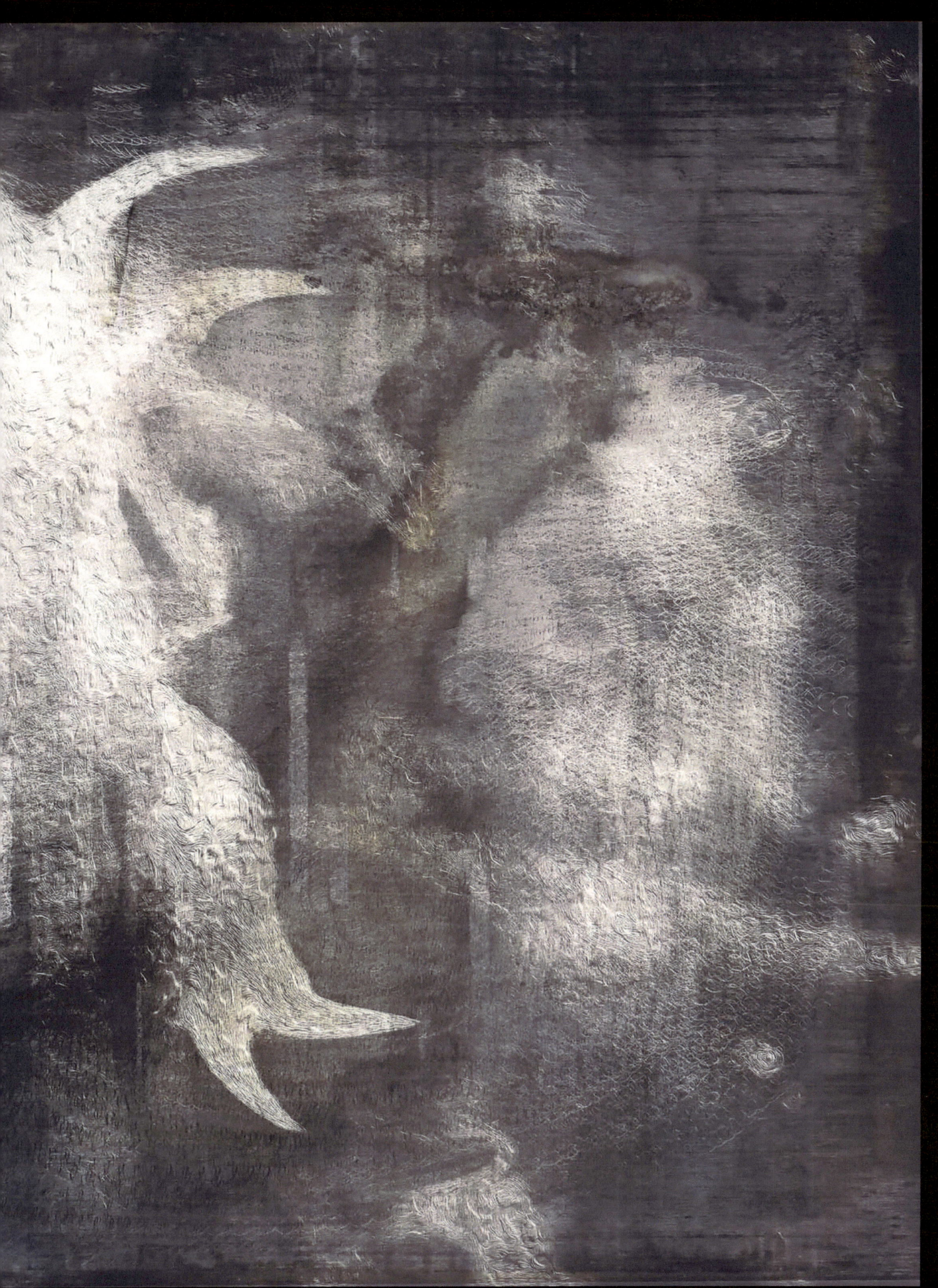

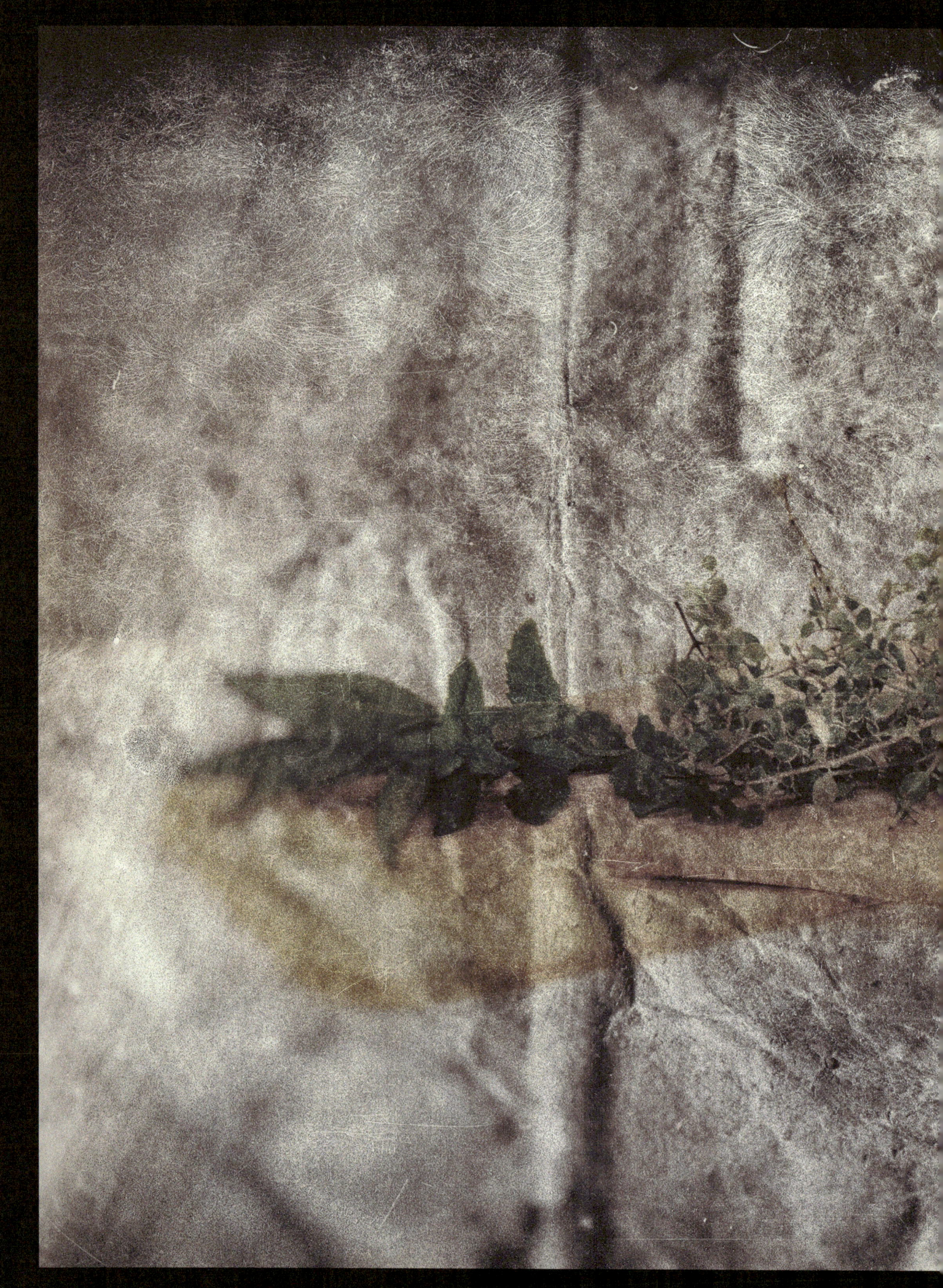

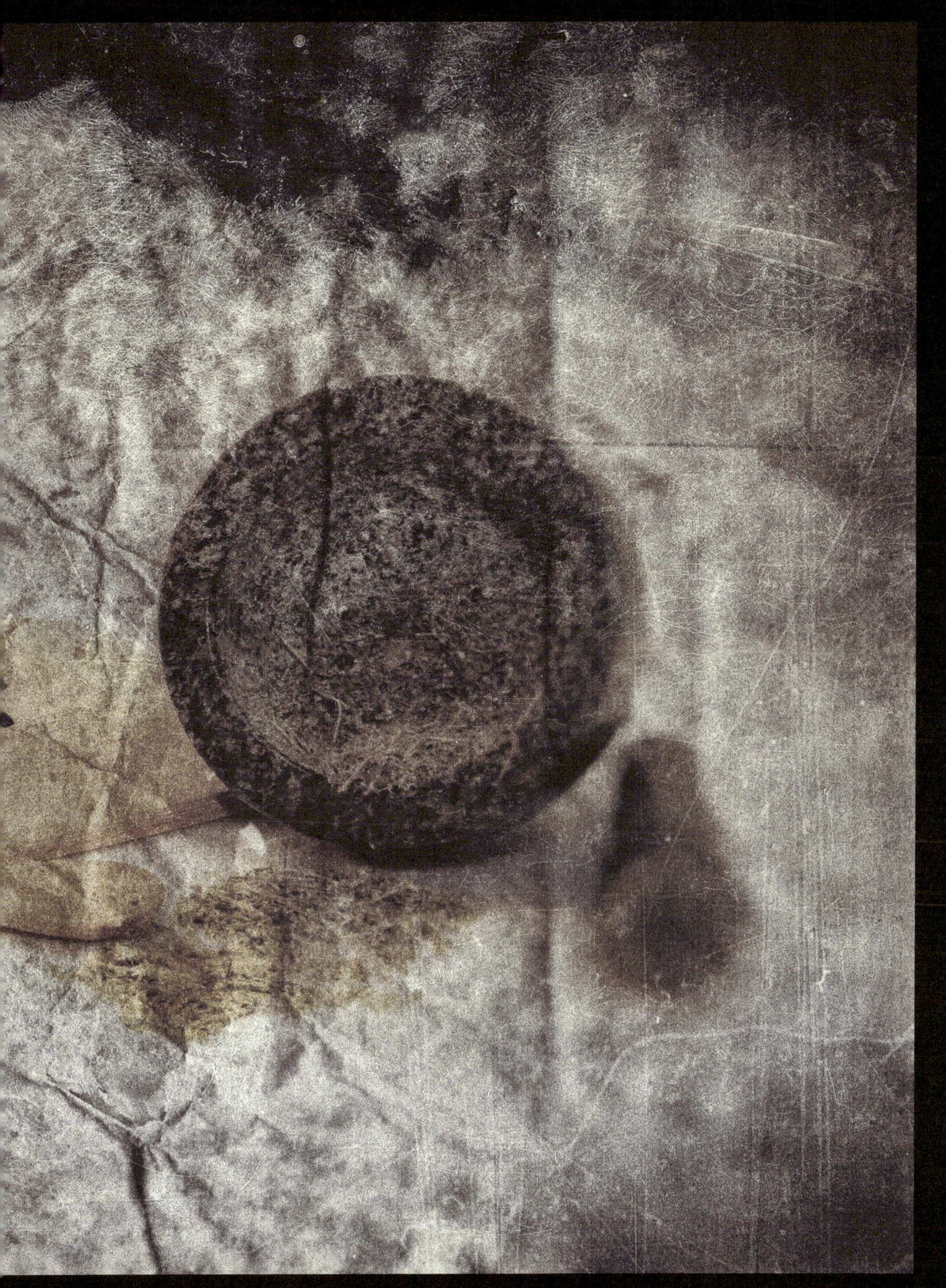

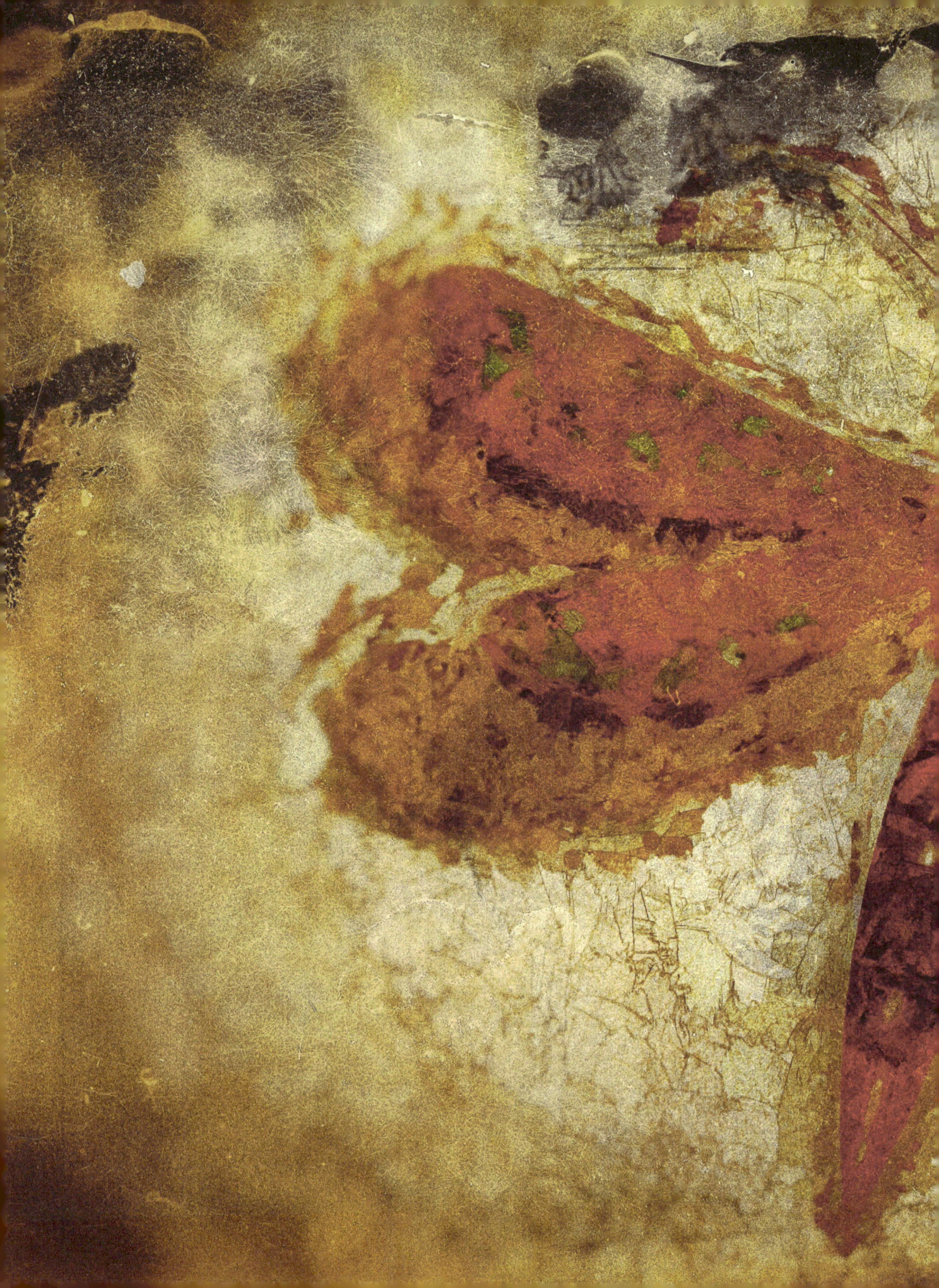

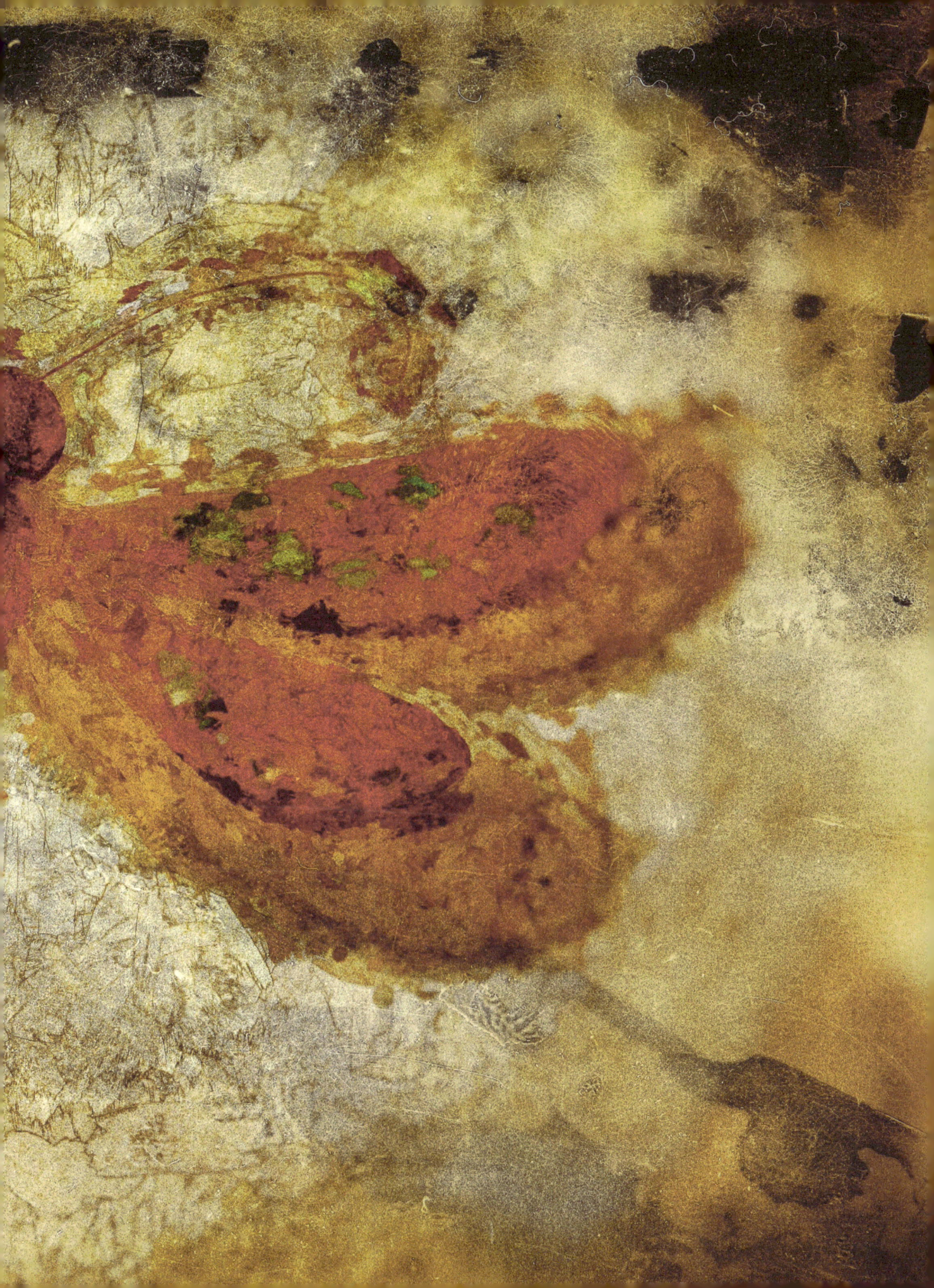

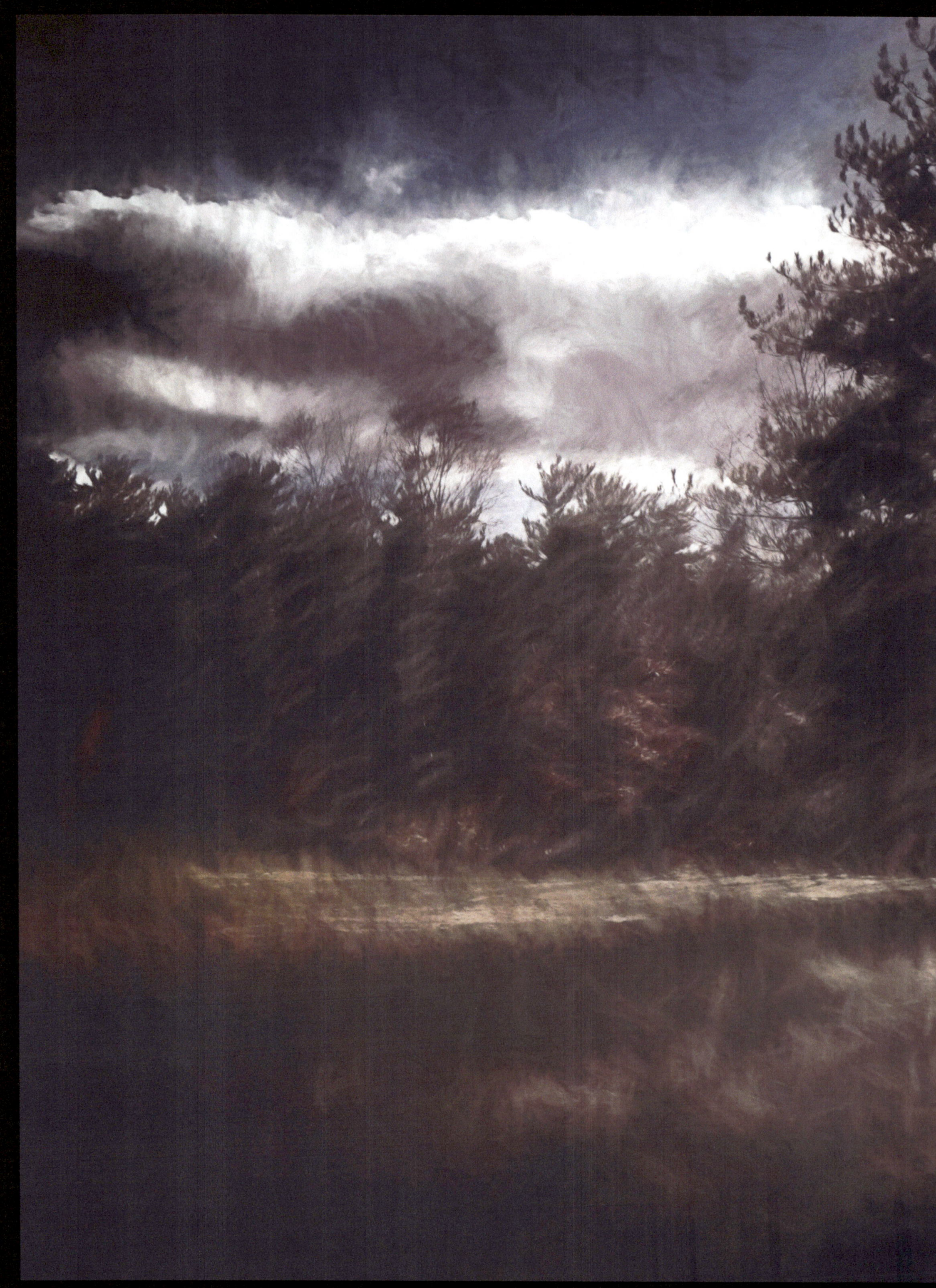

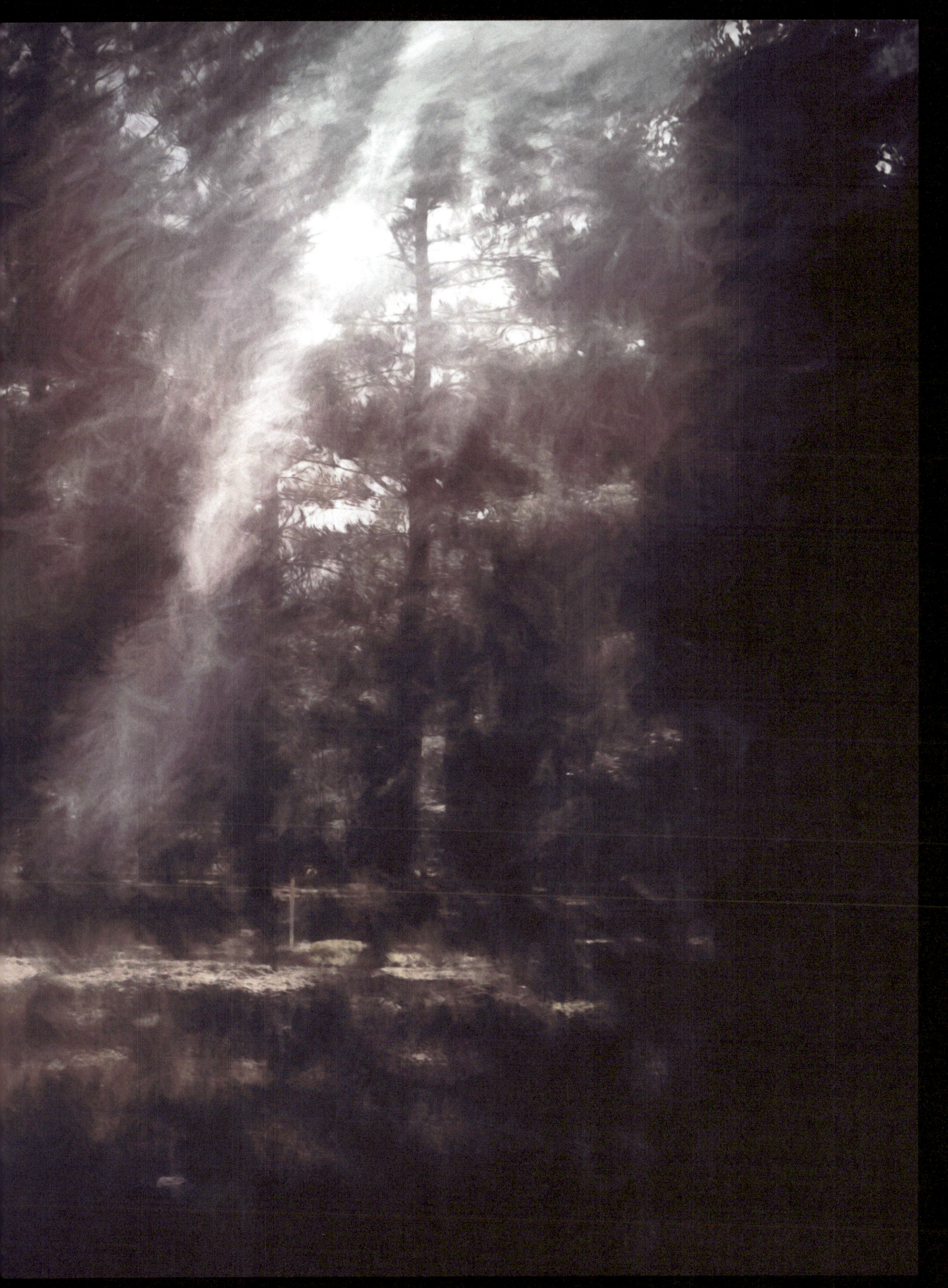

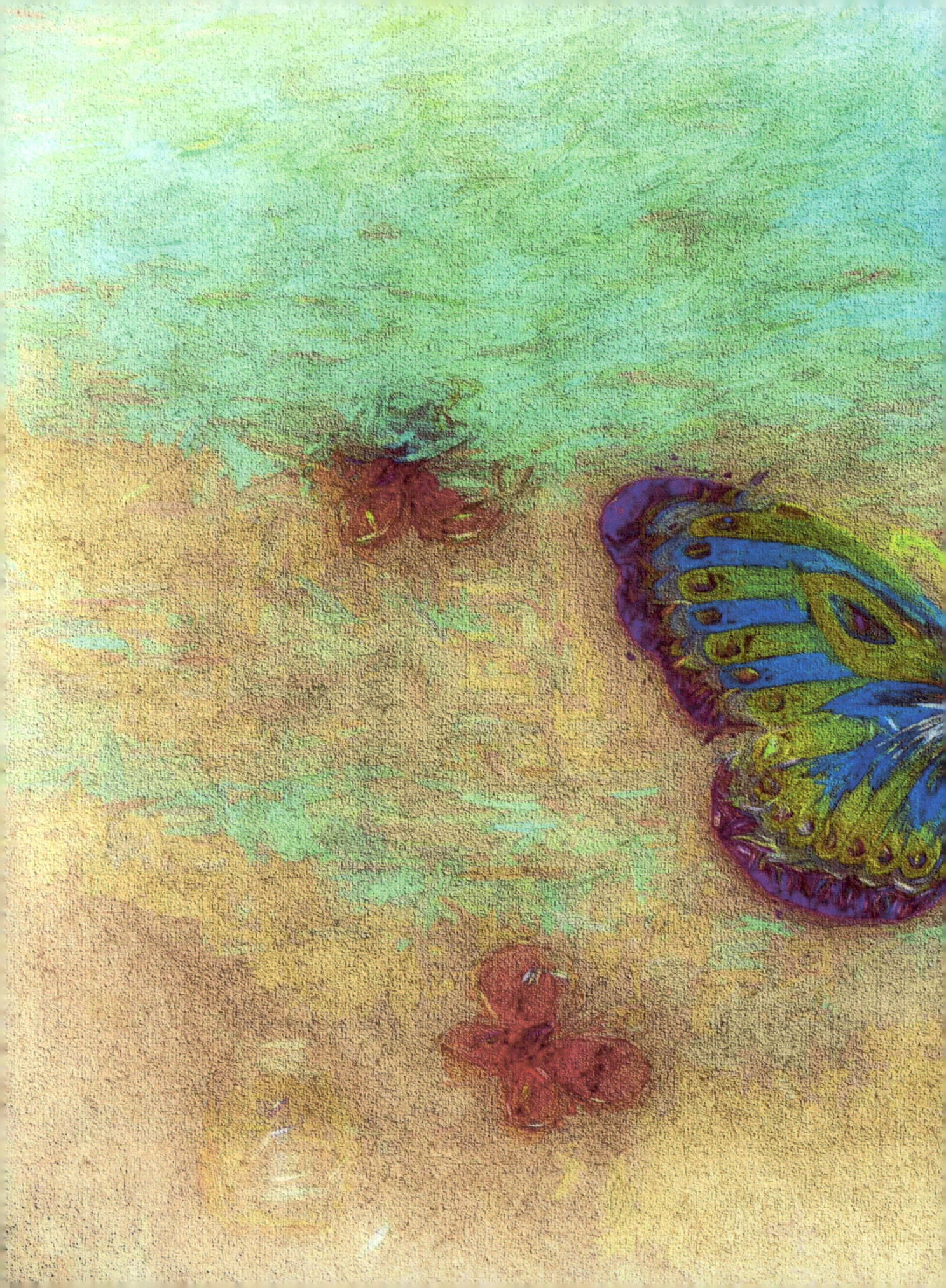

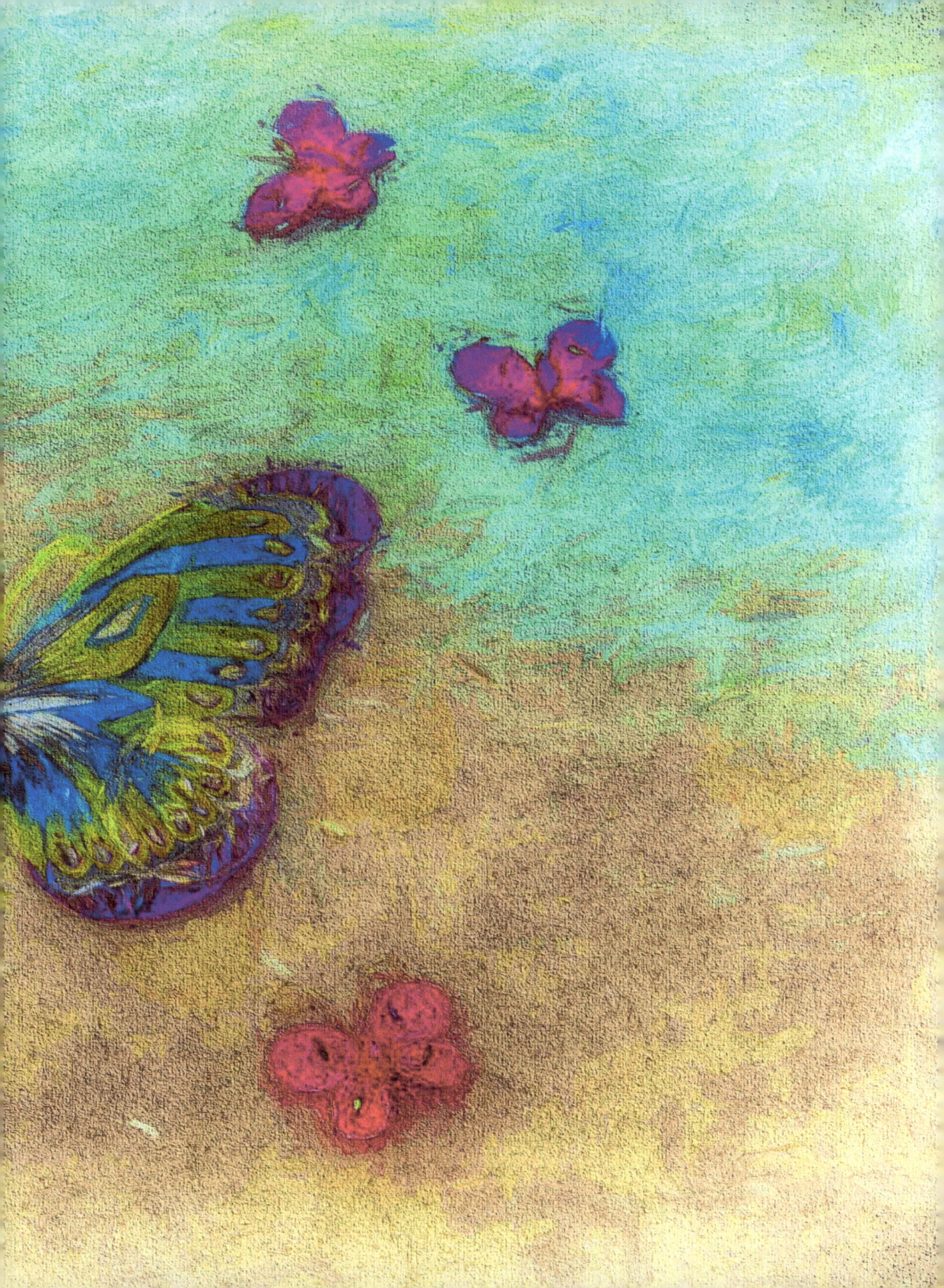

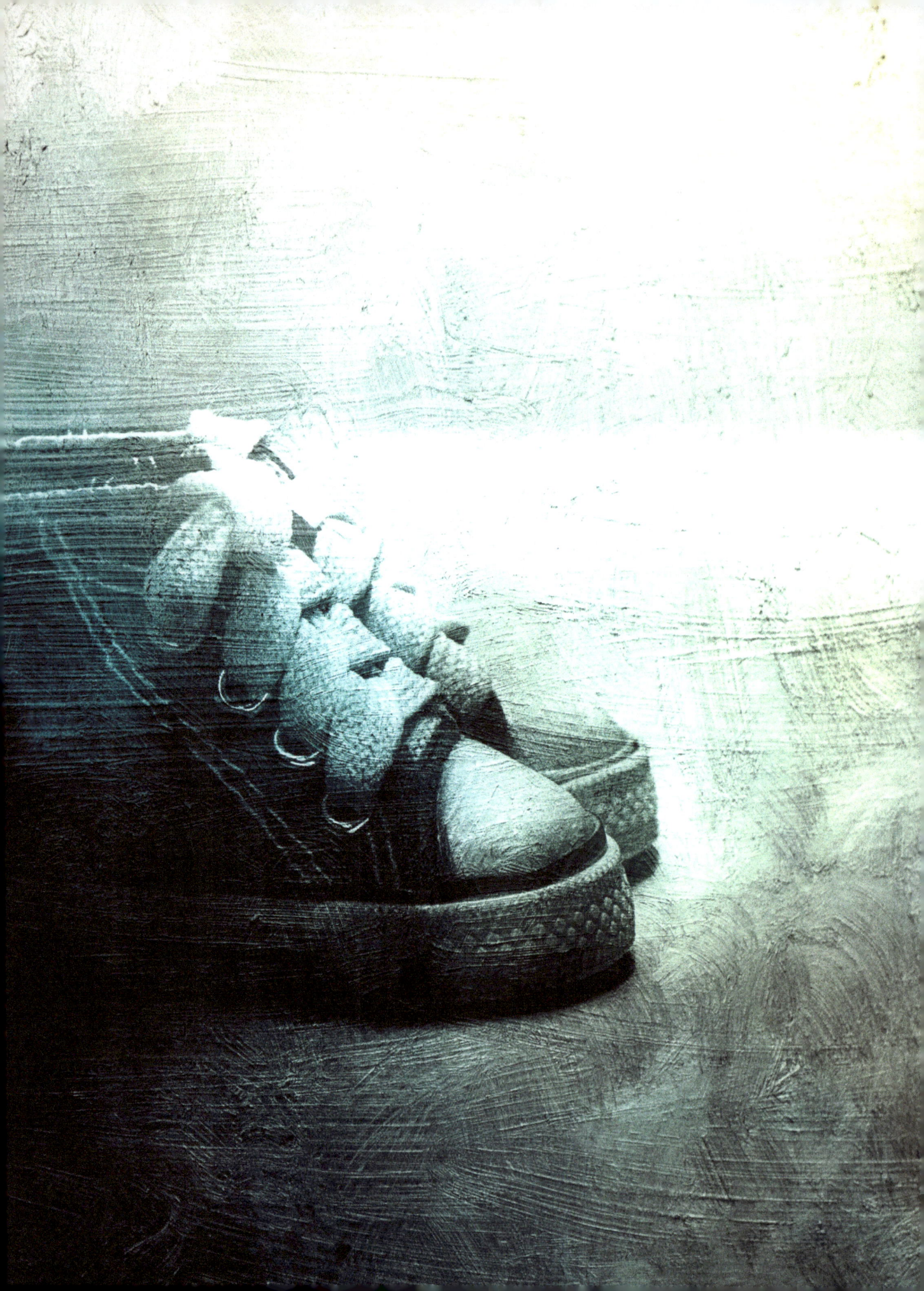

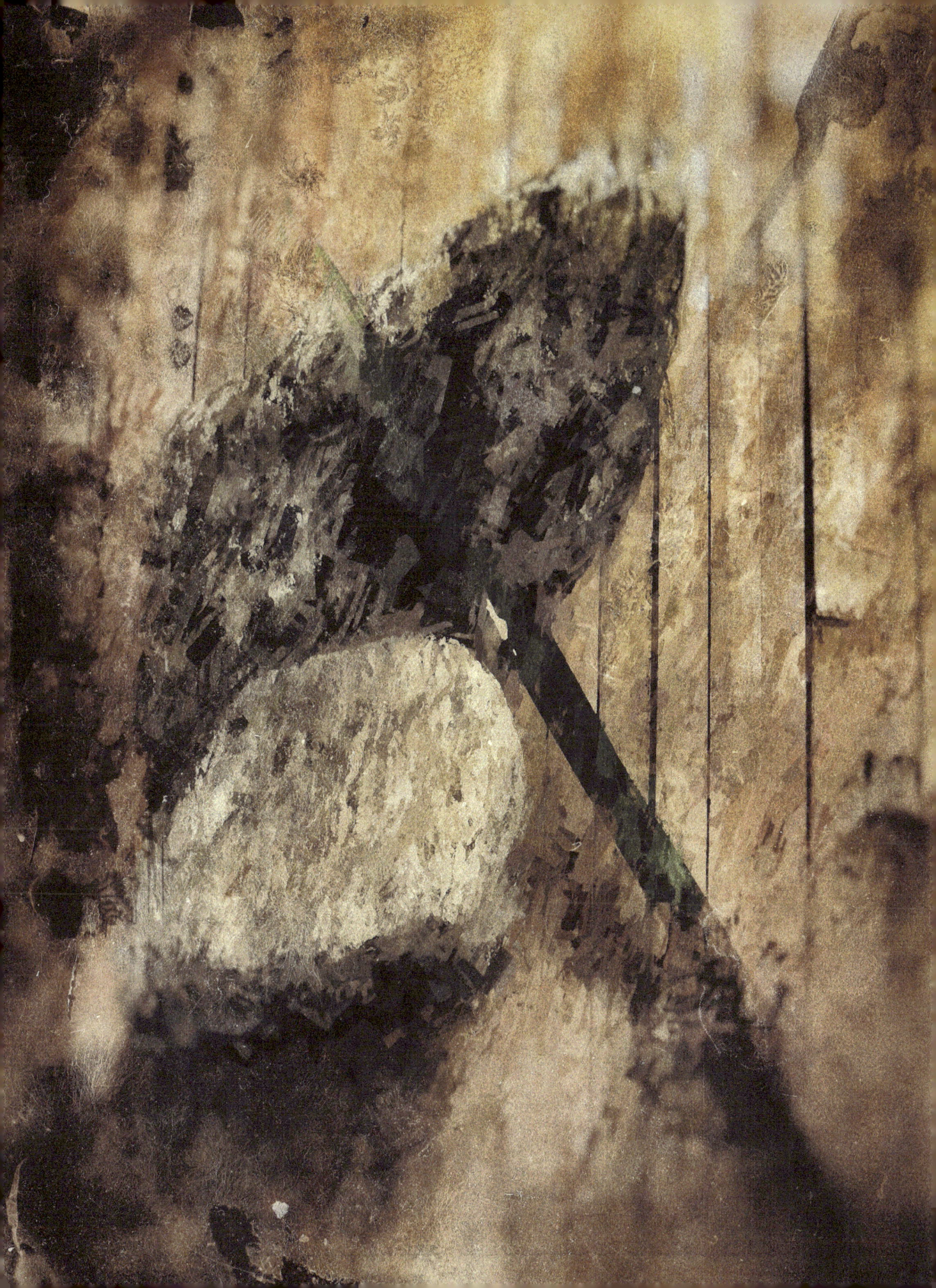

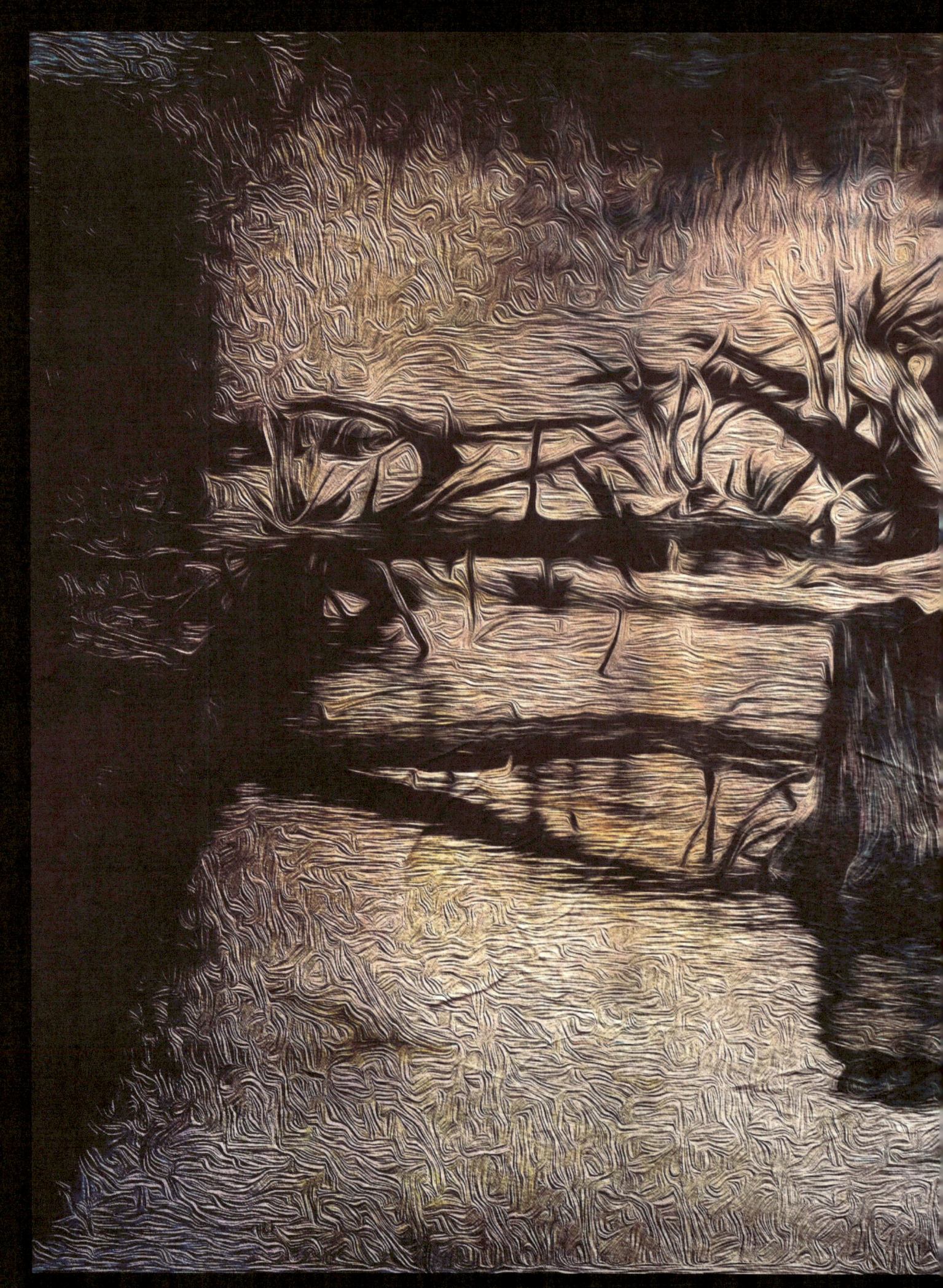

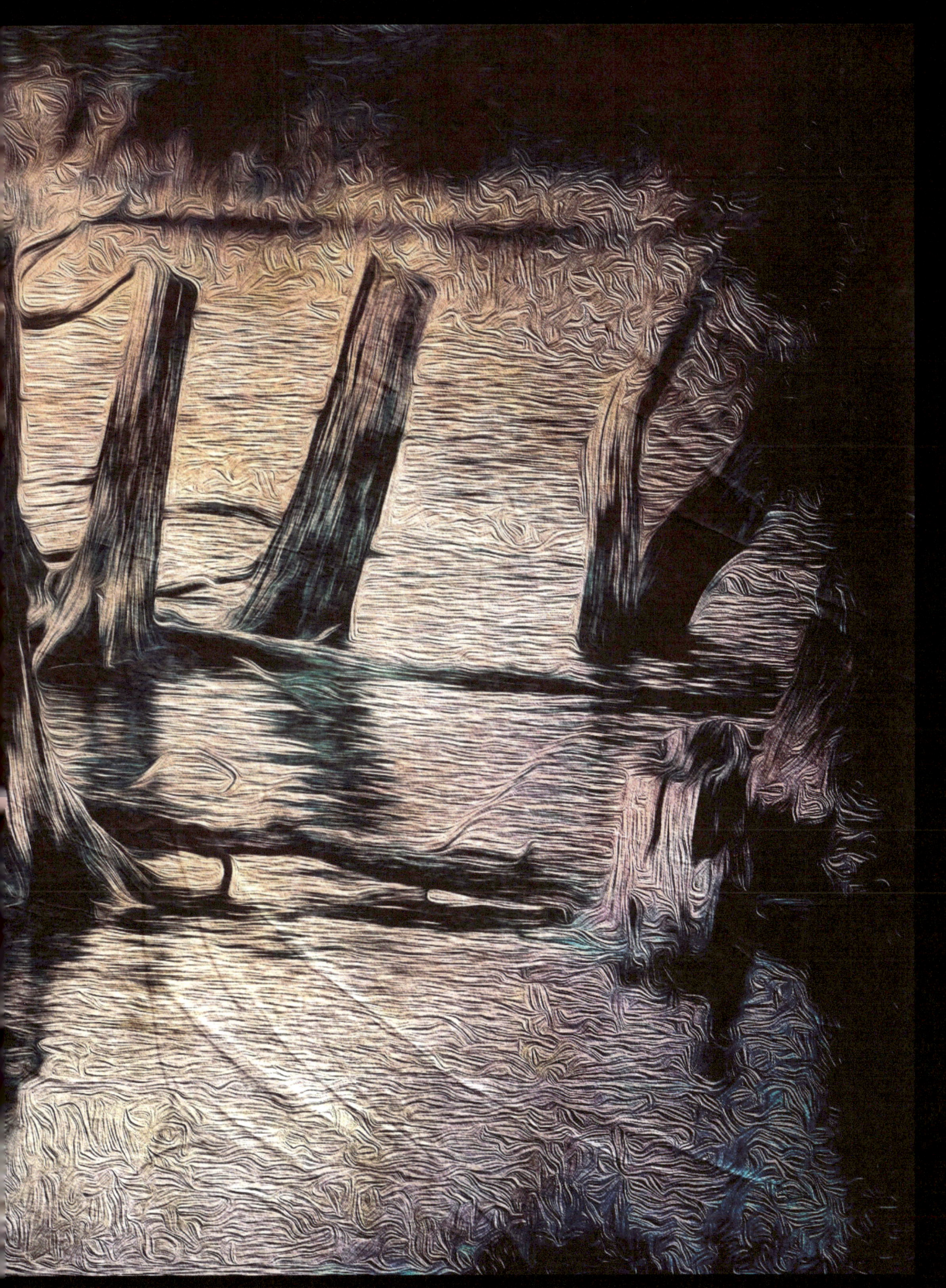

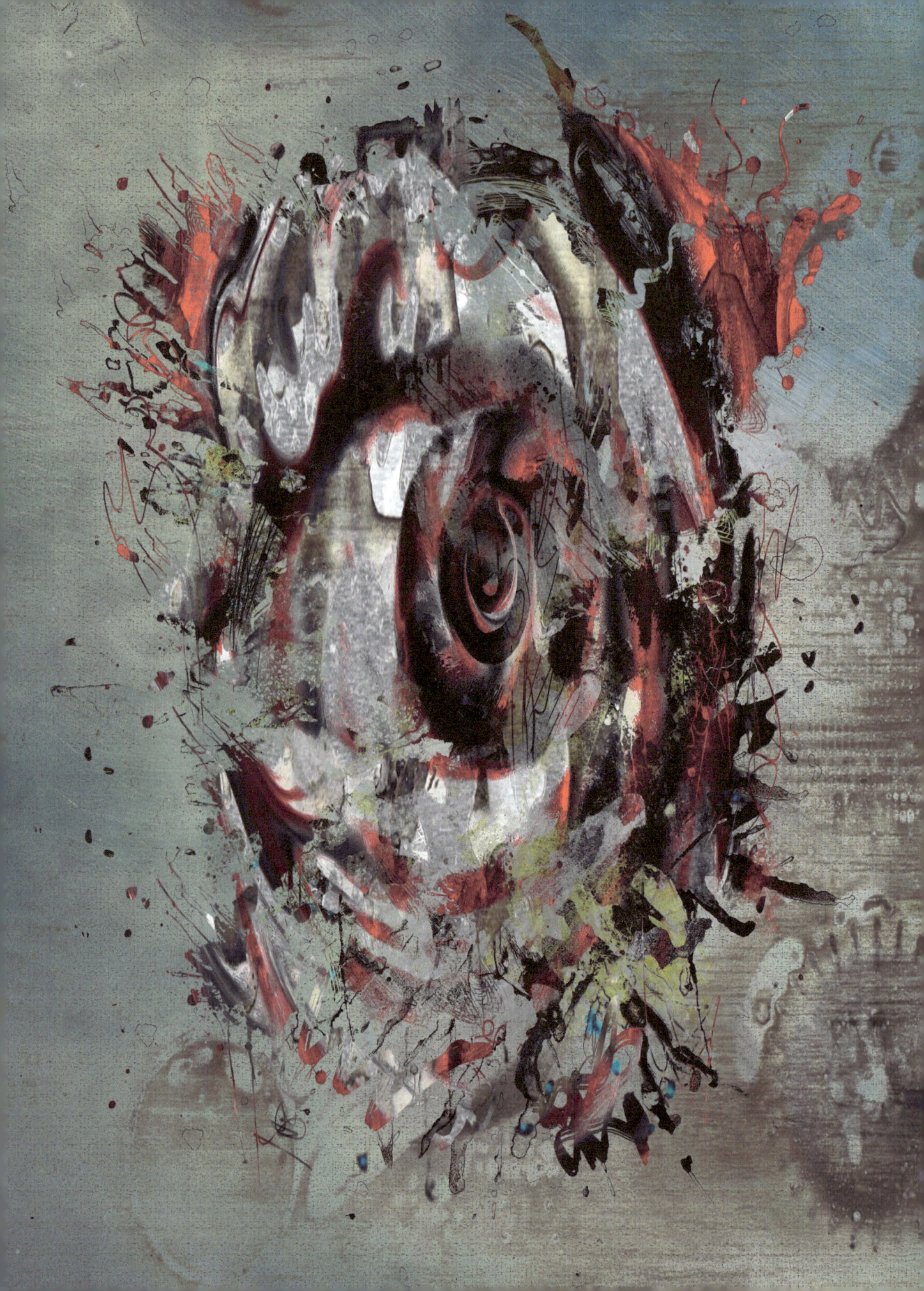

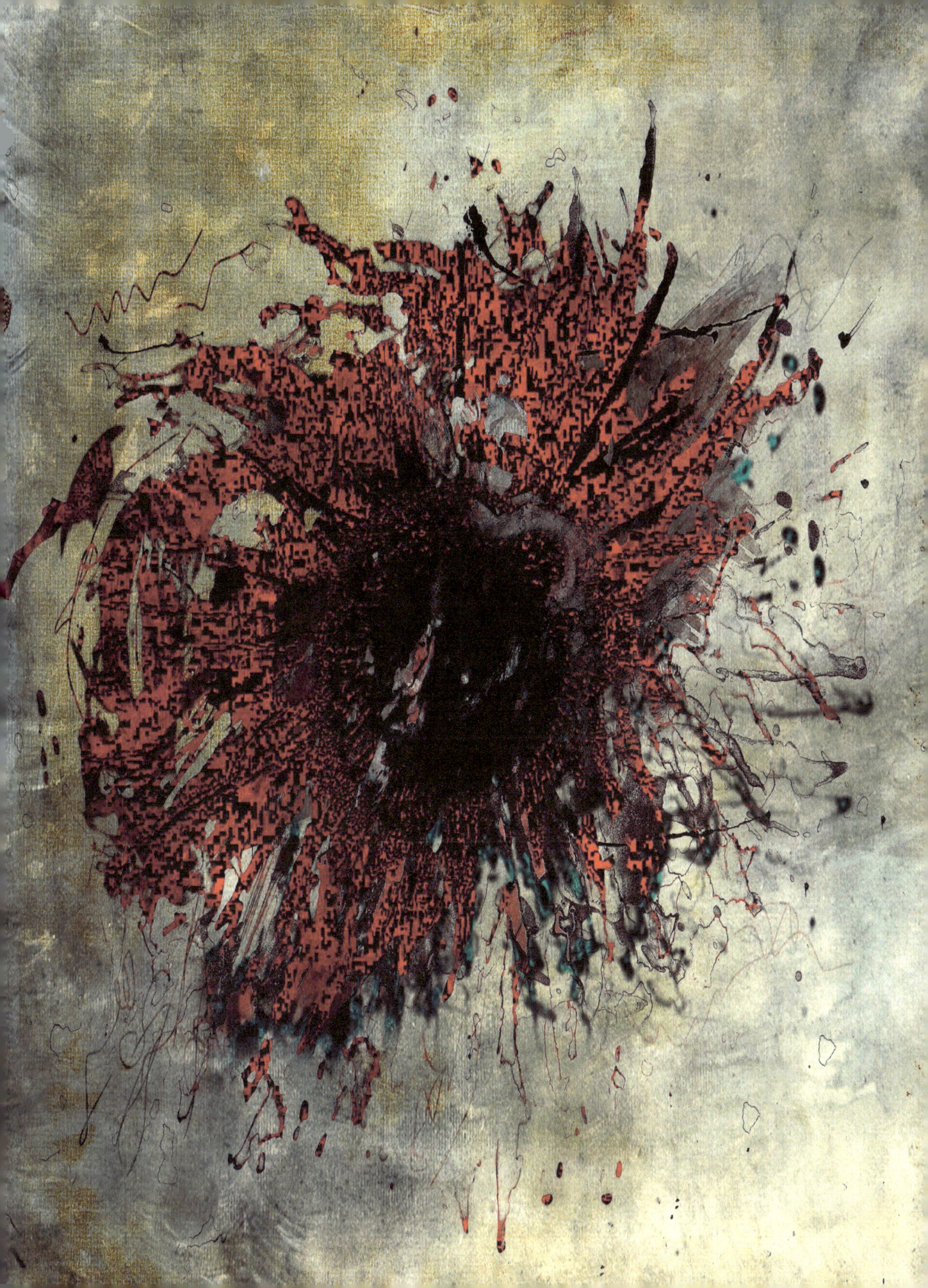

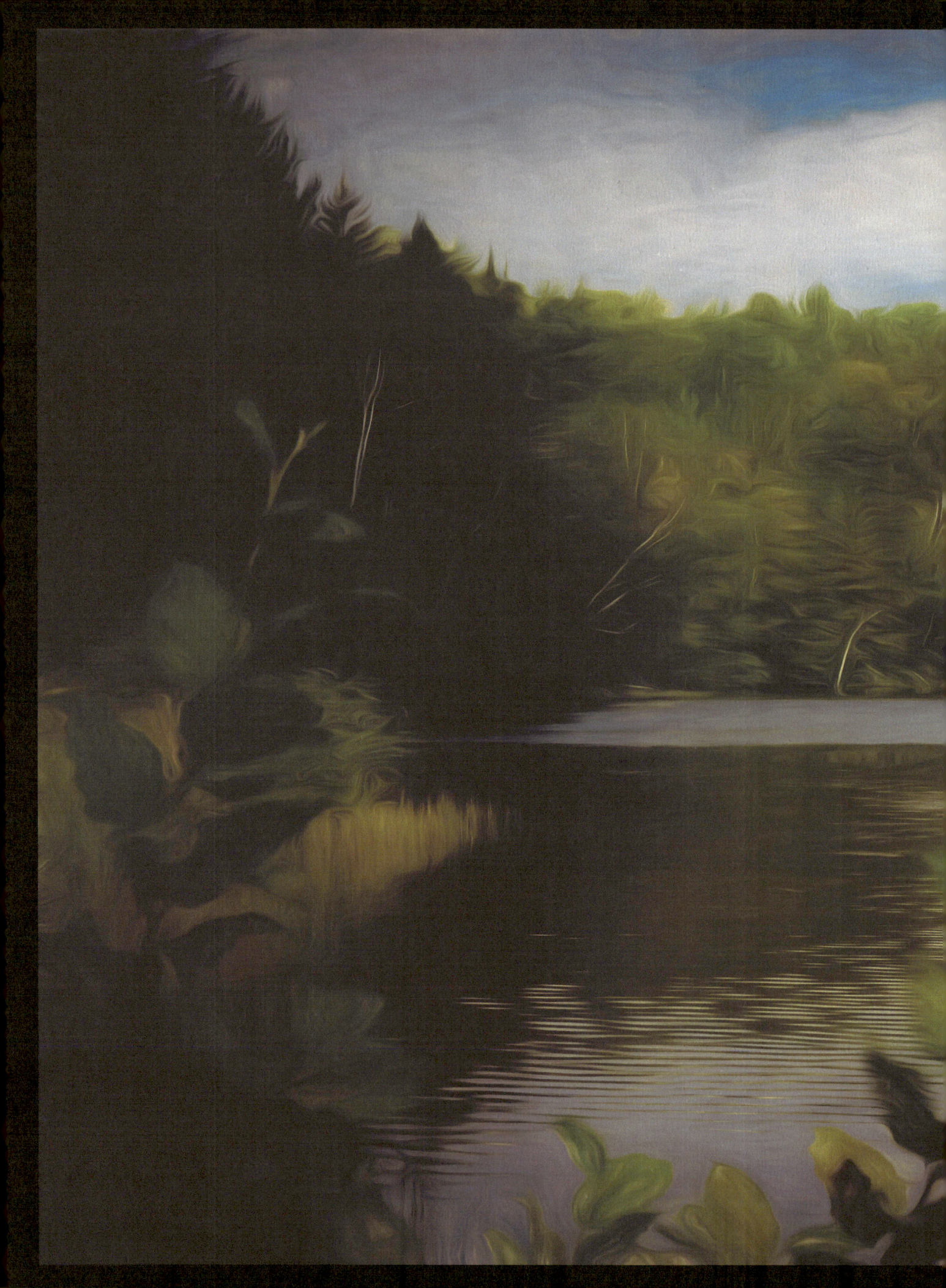

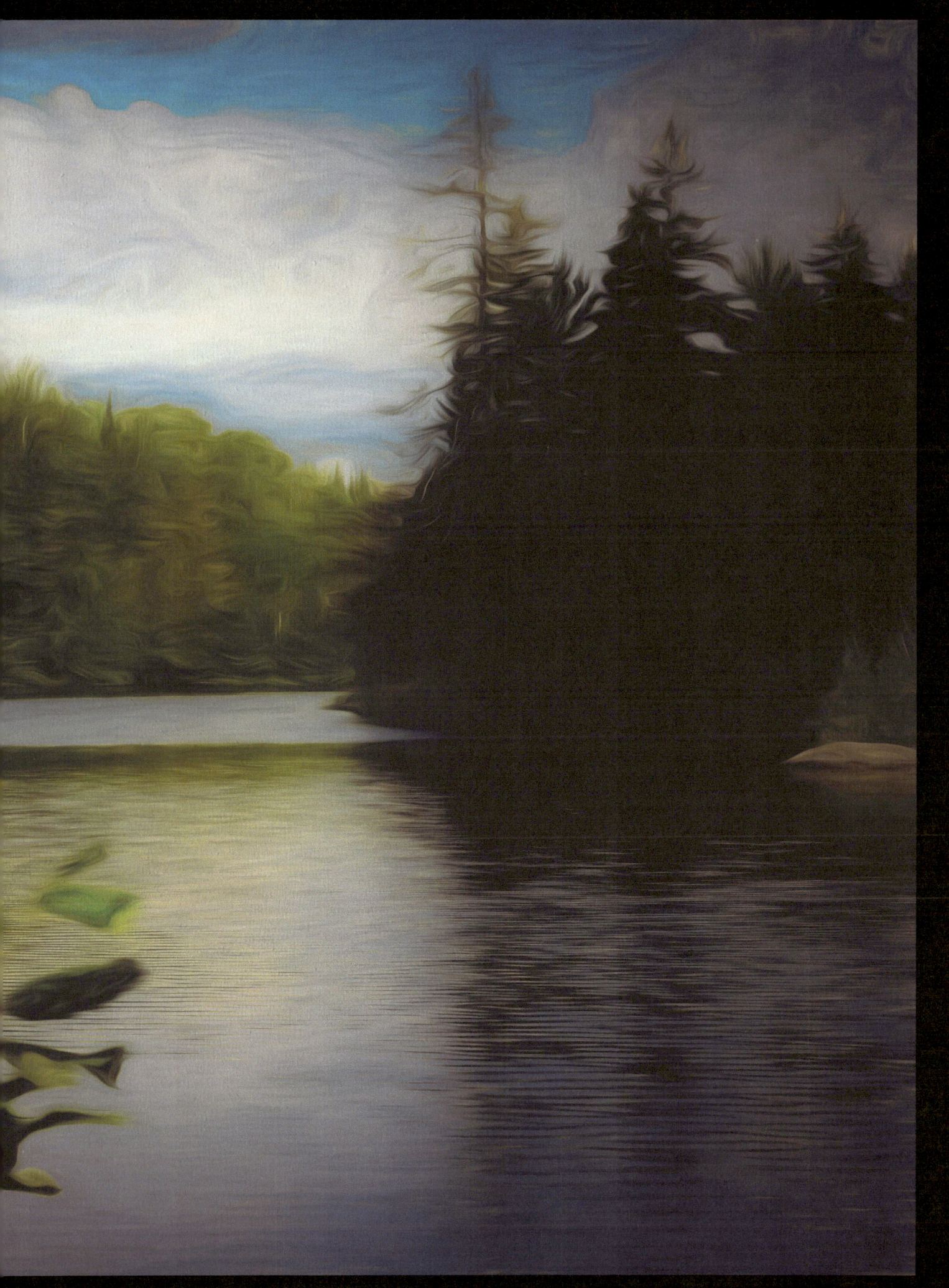

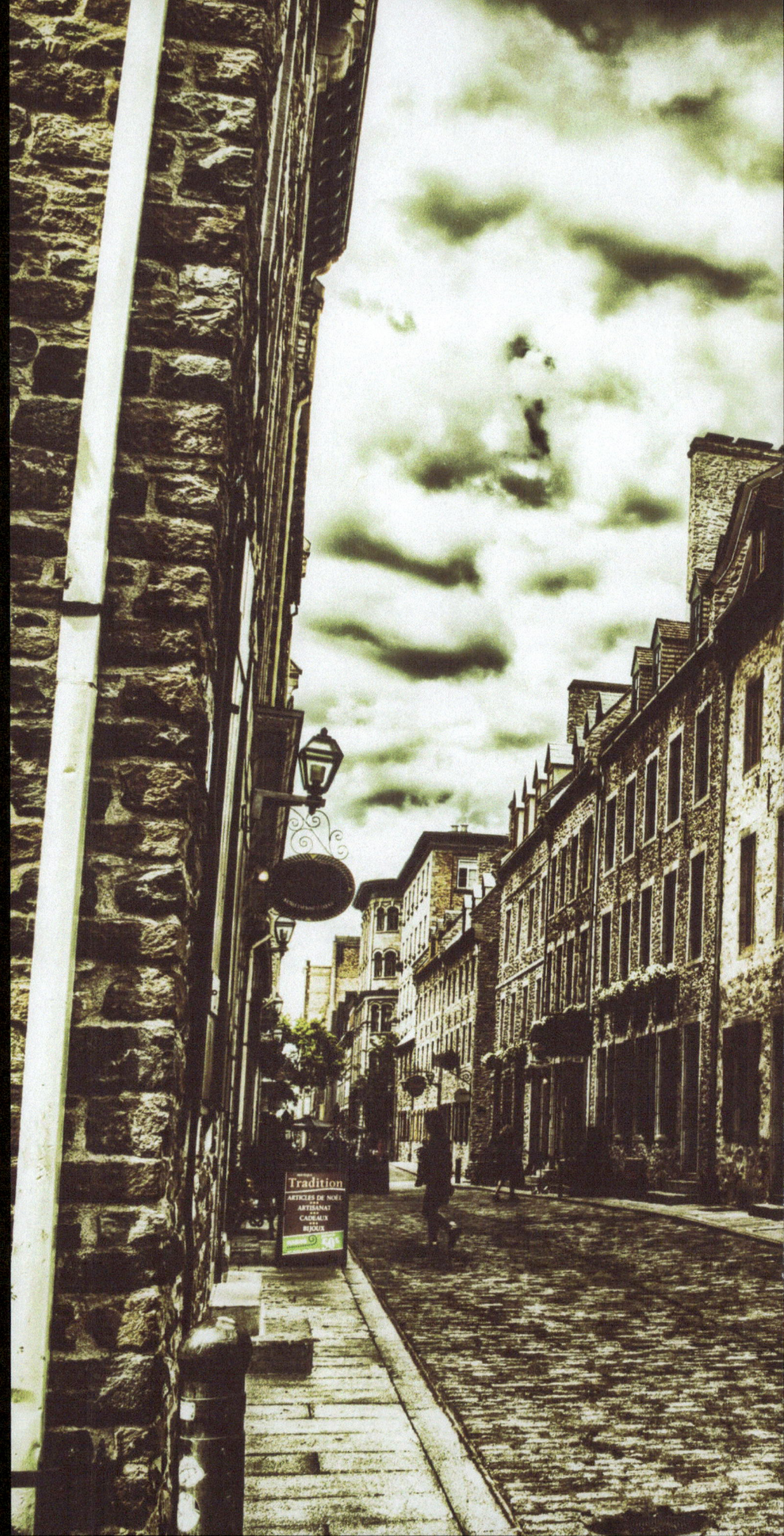

trip on Québec
city

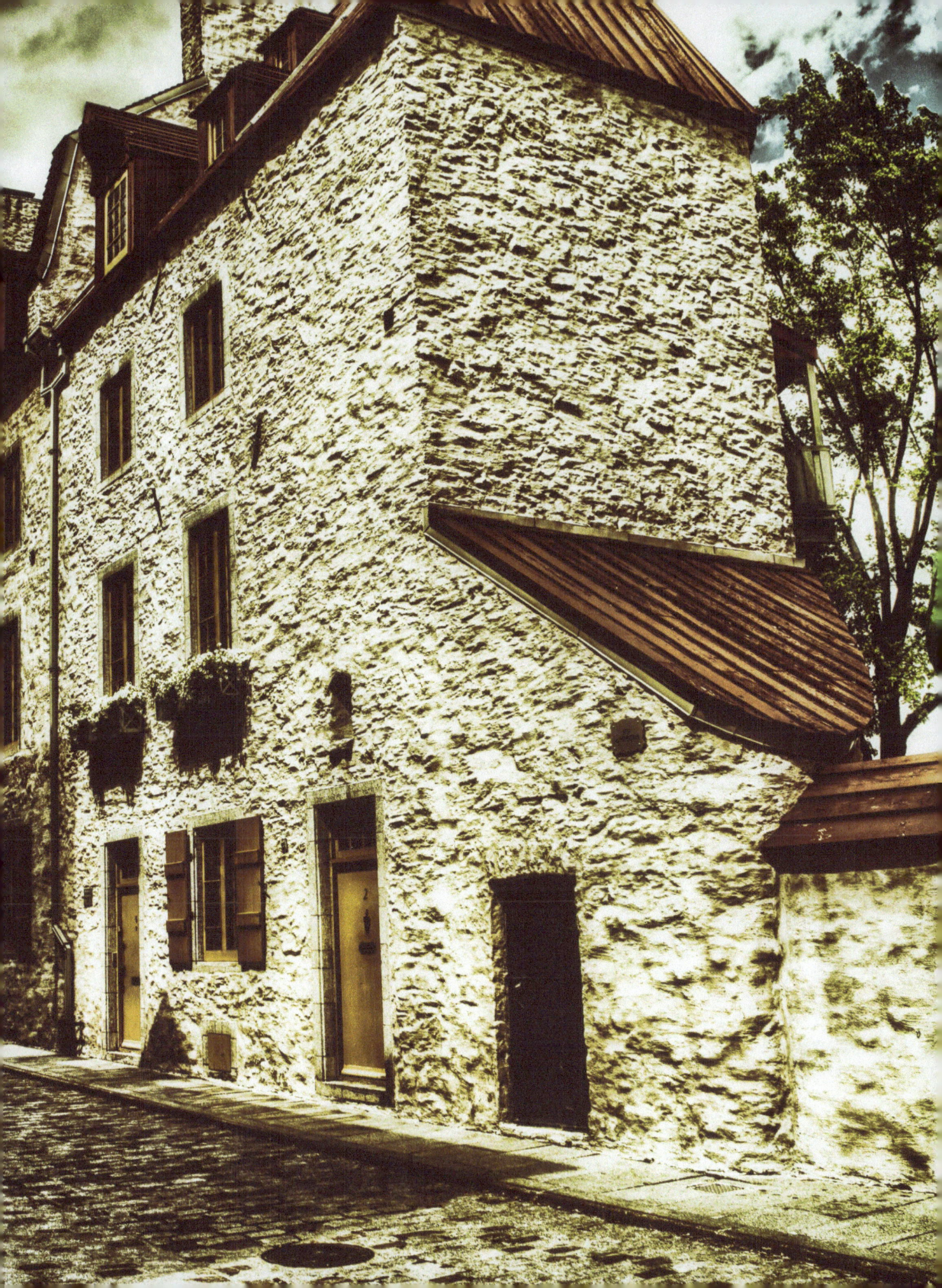

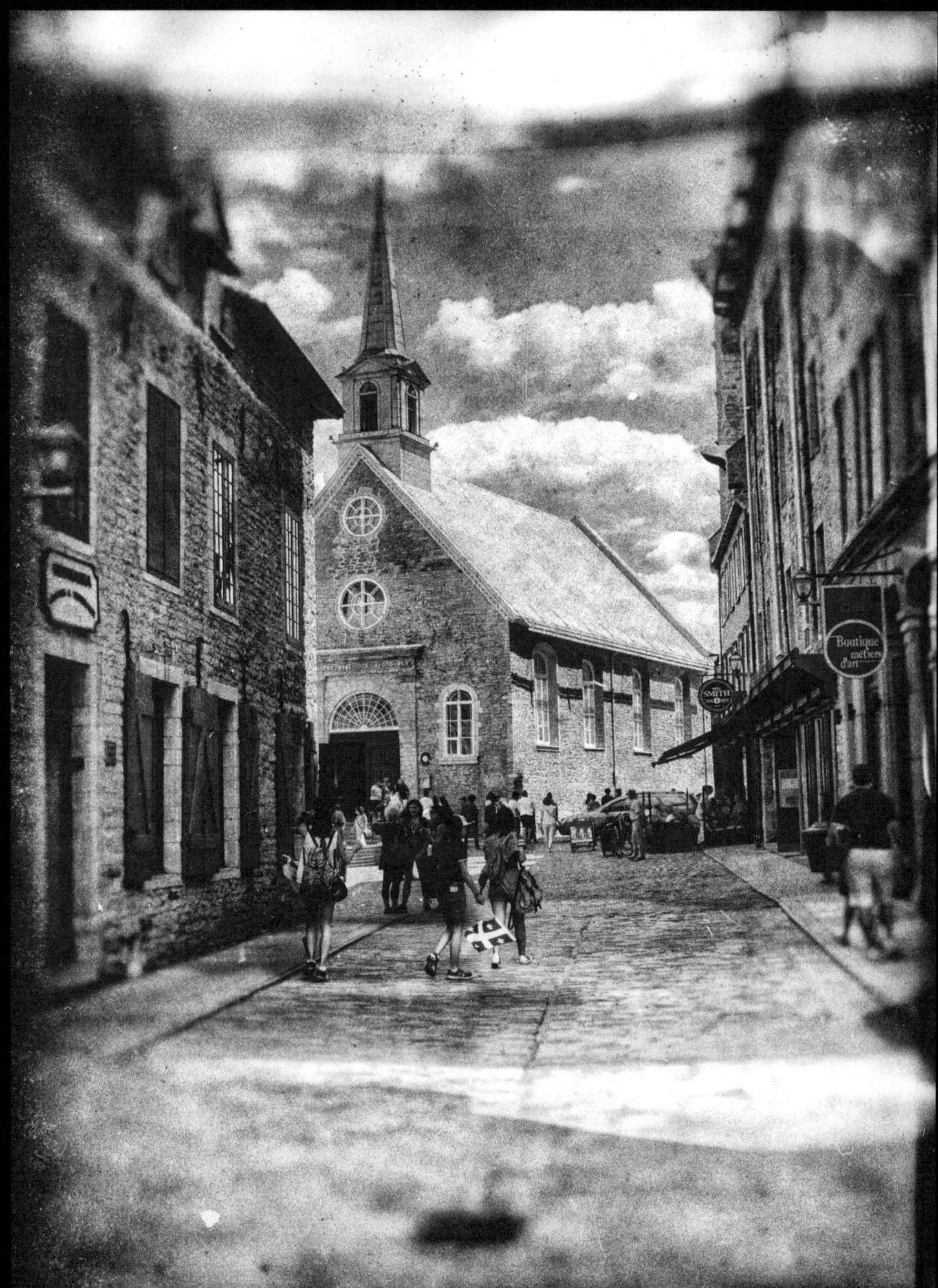

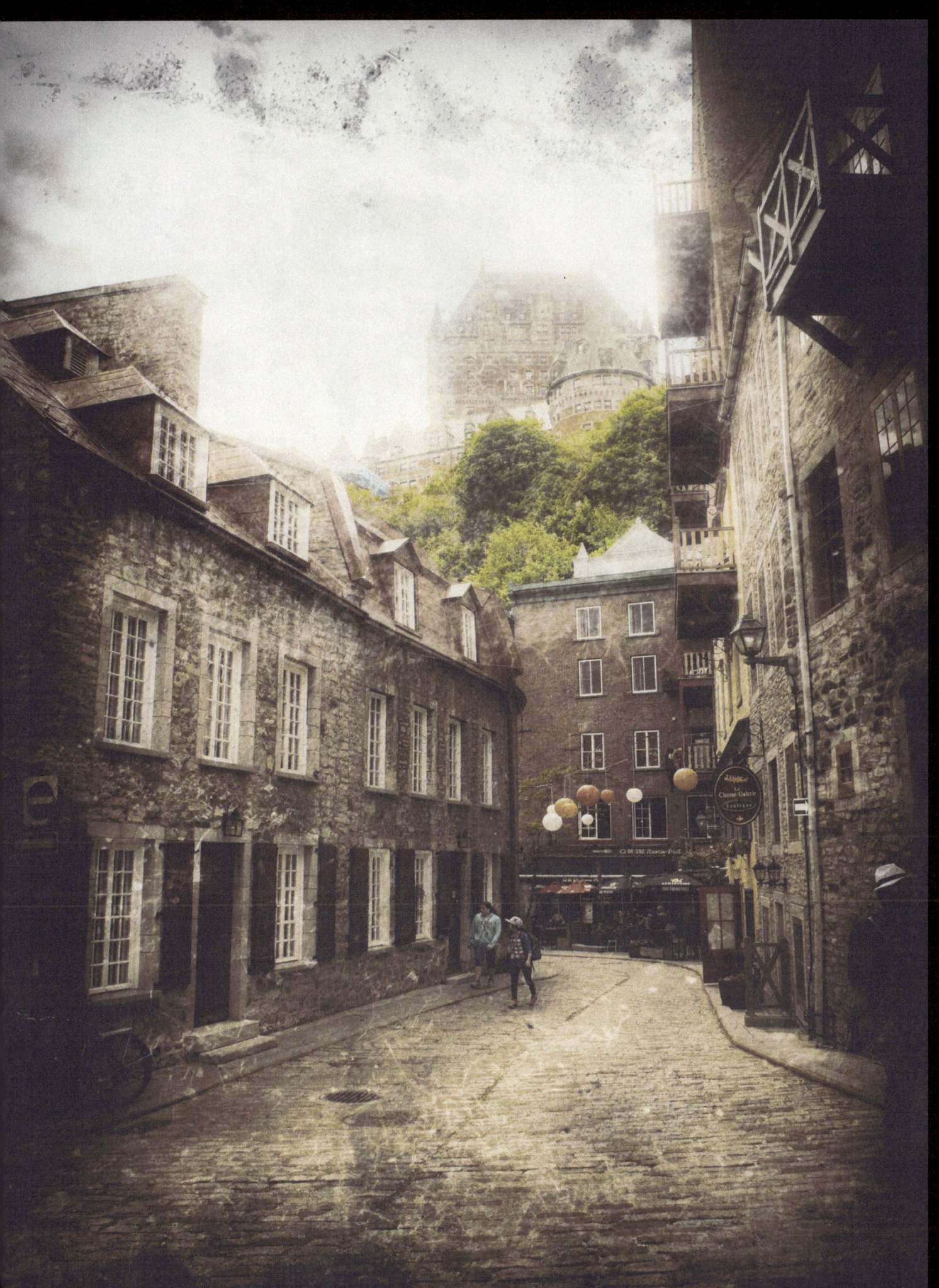

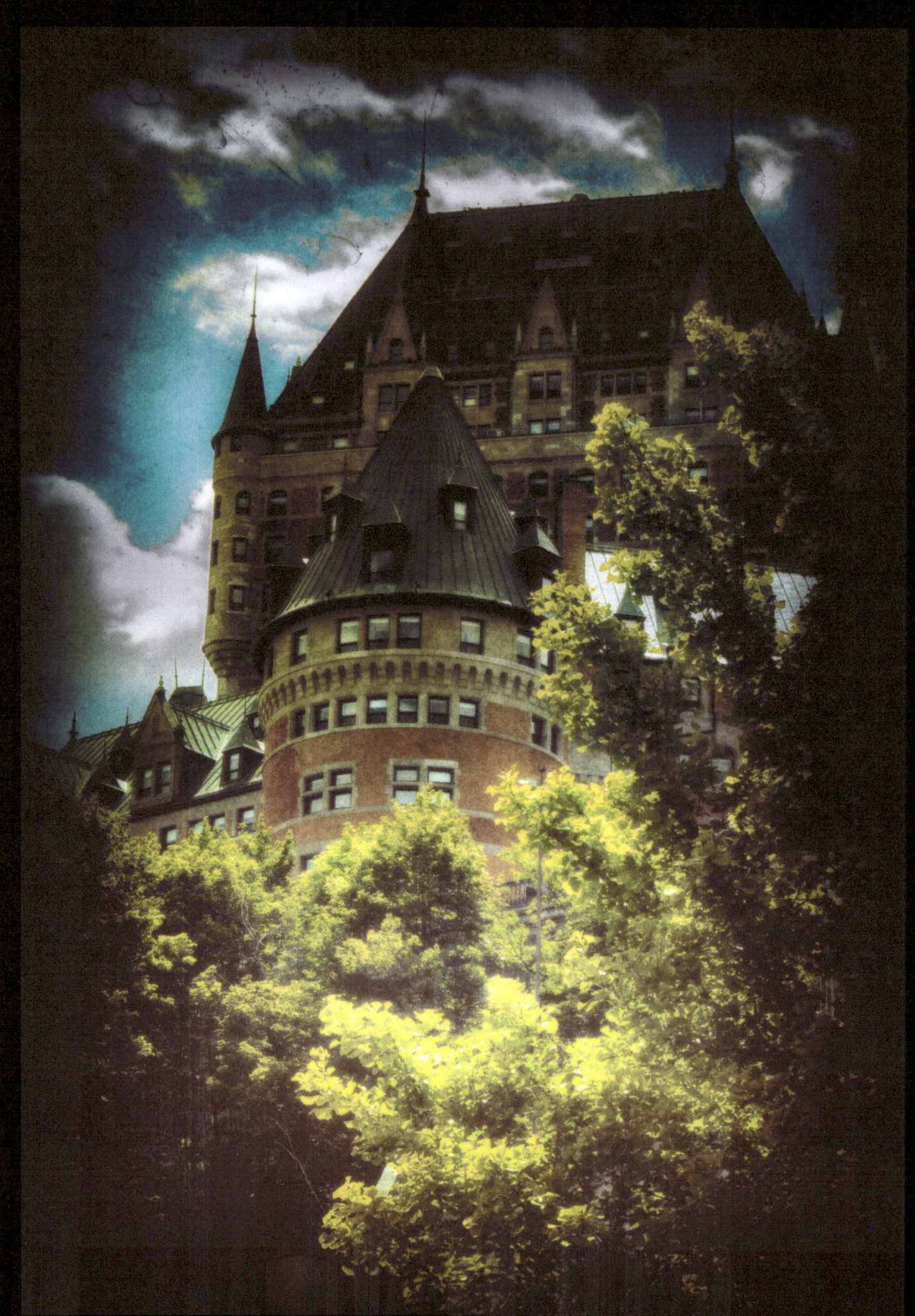

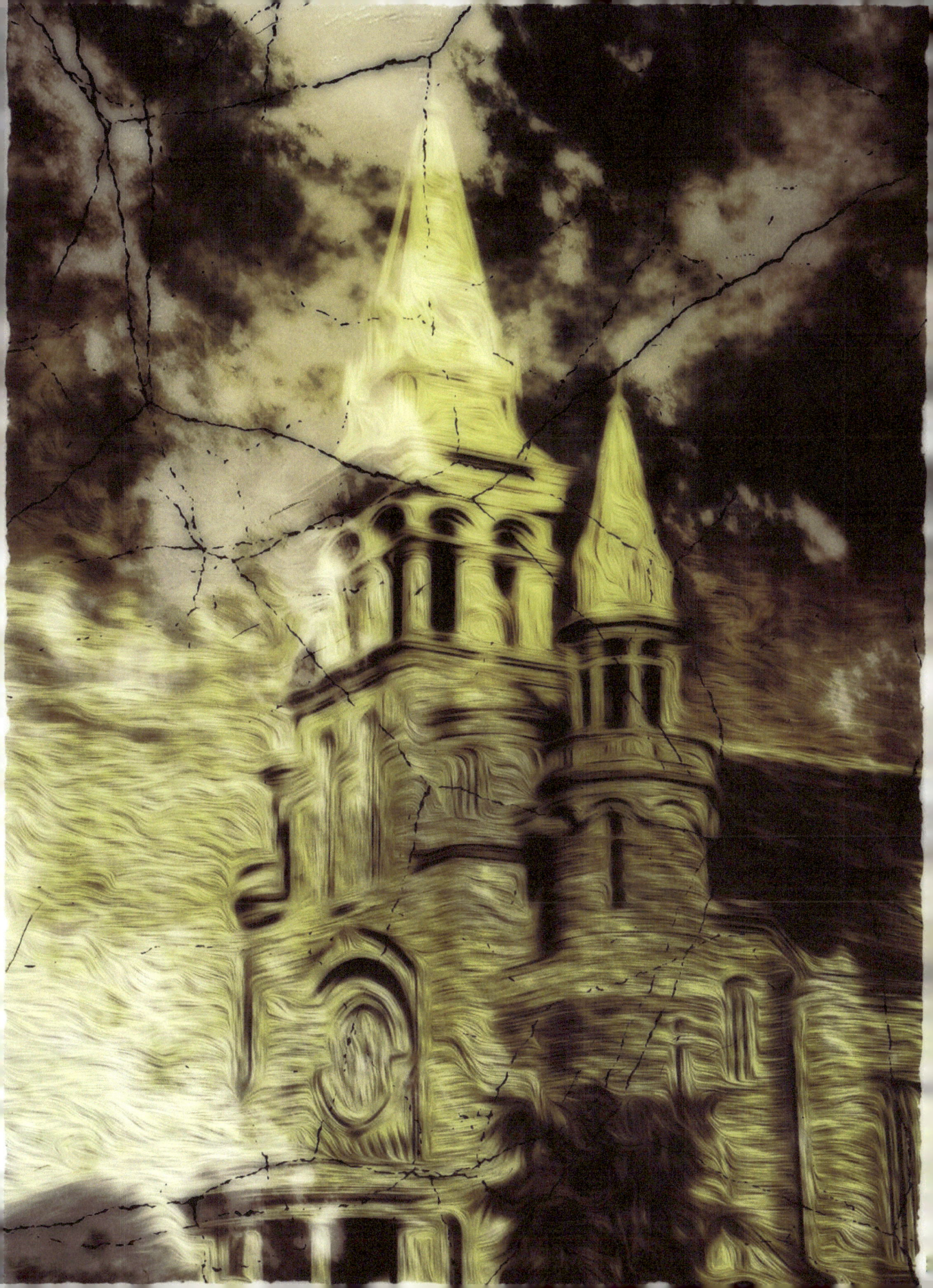

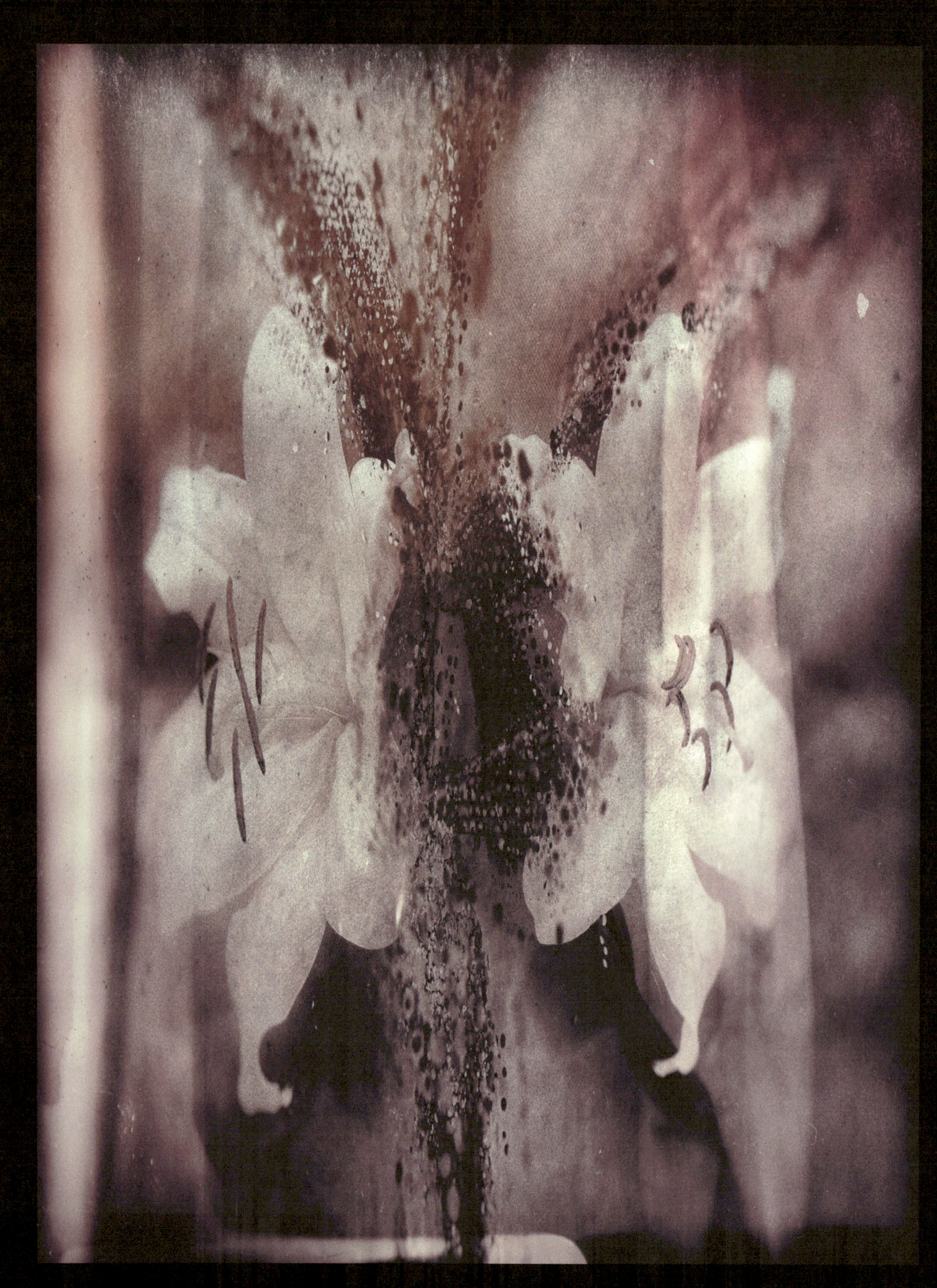

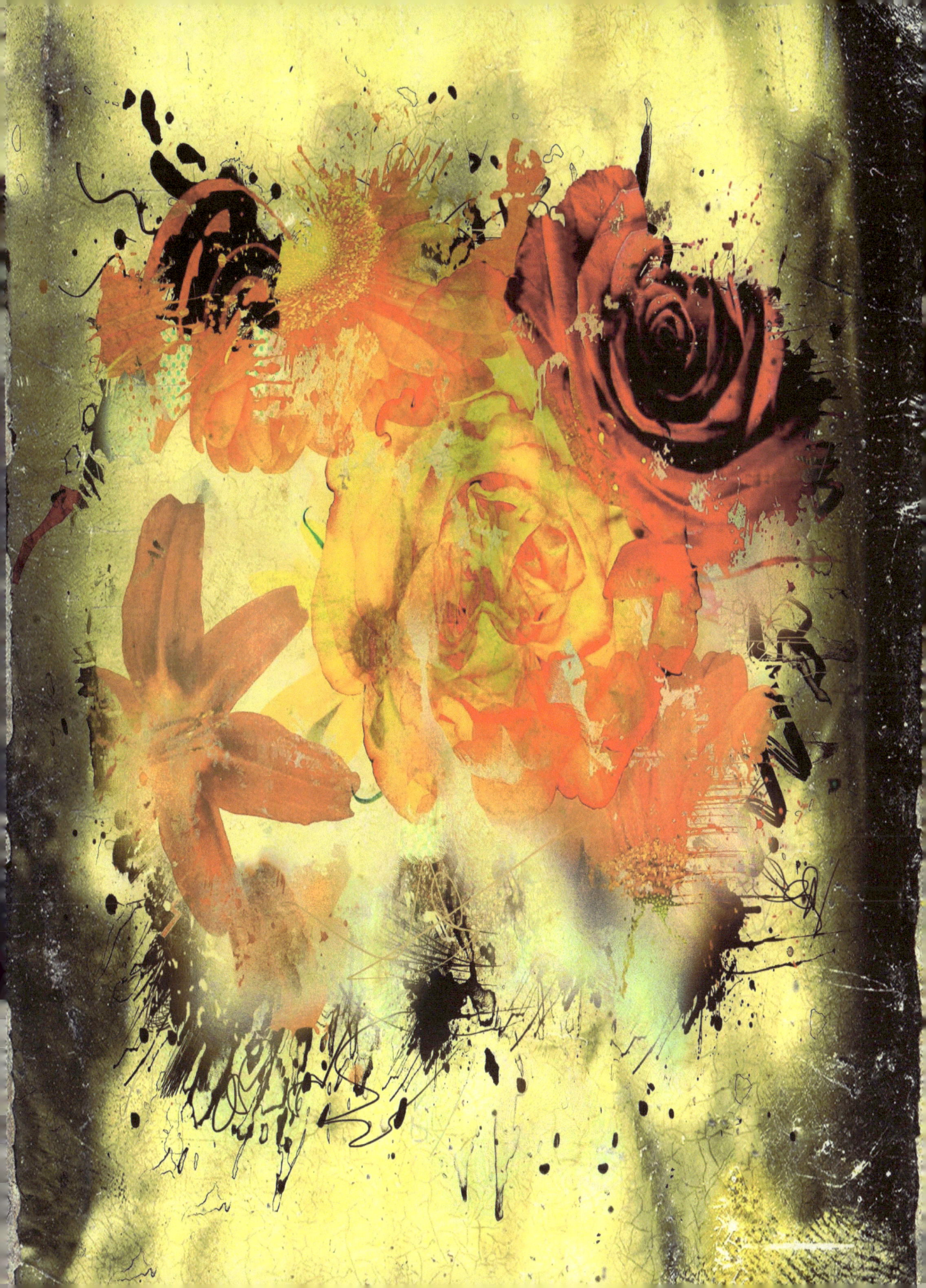

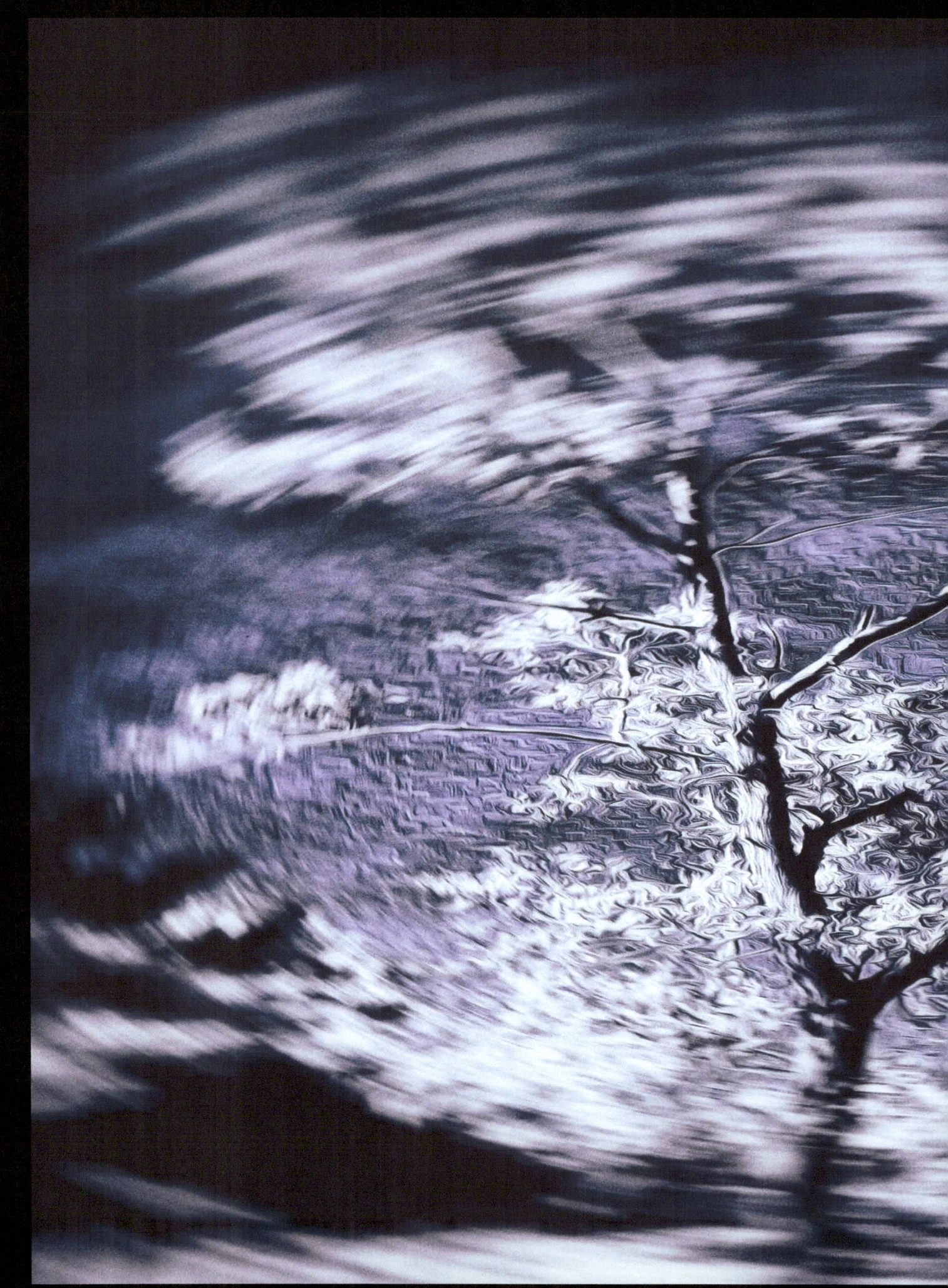

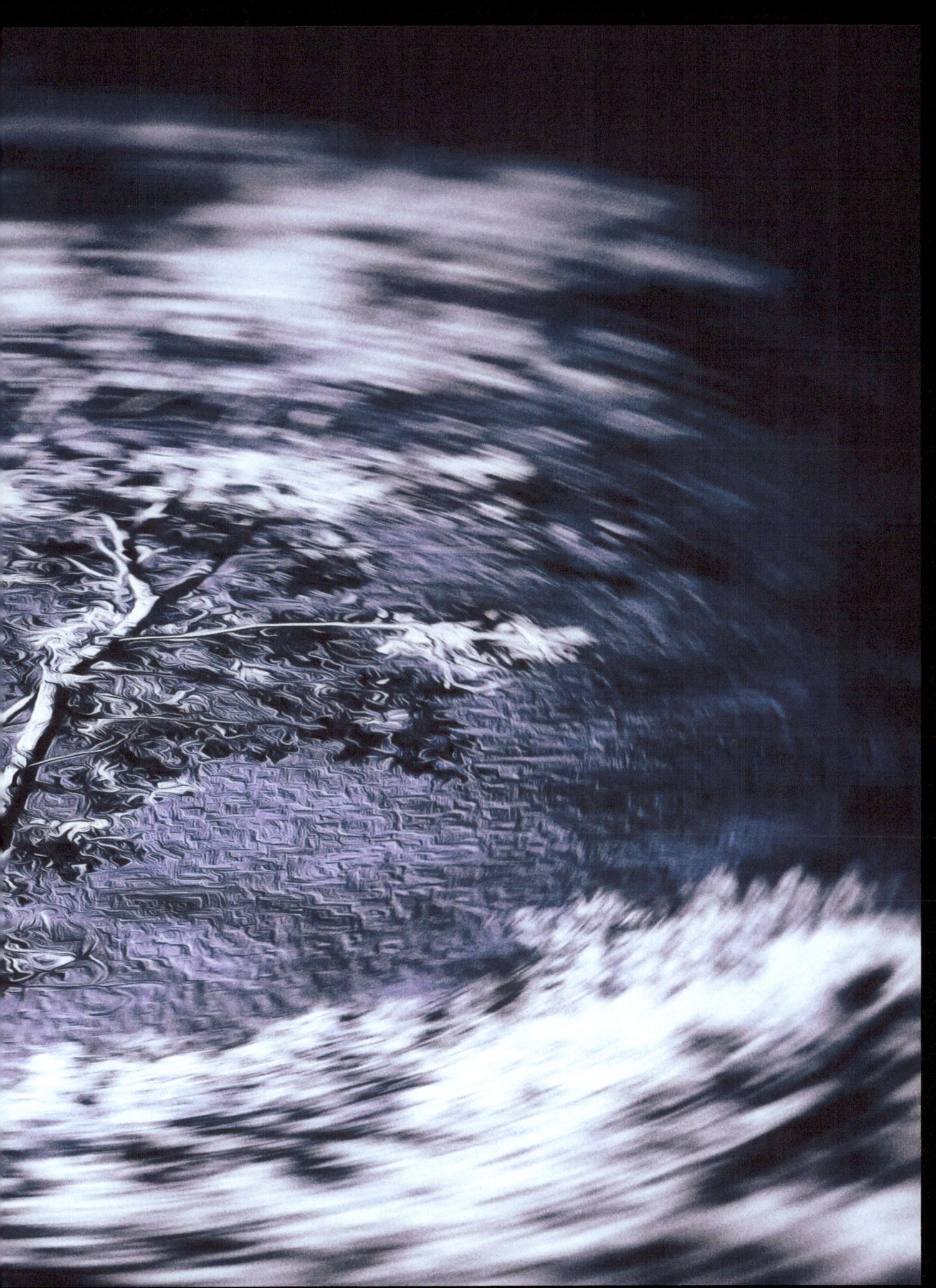

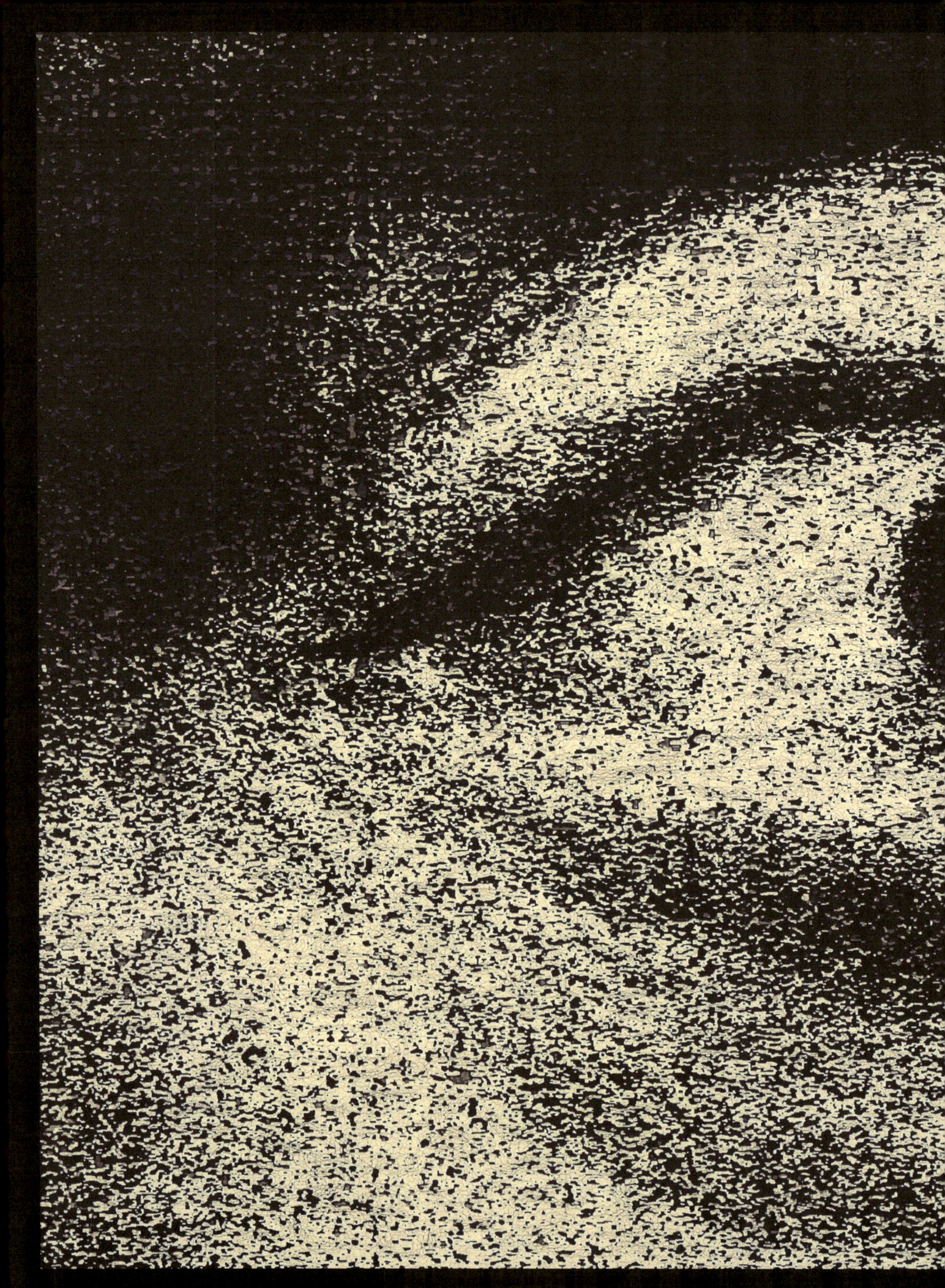

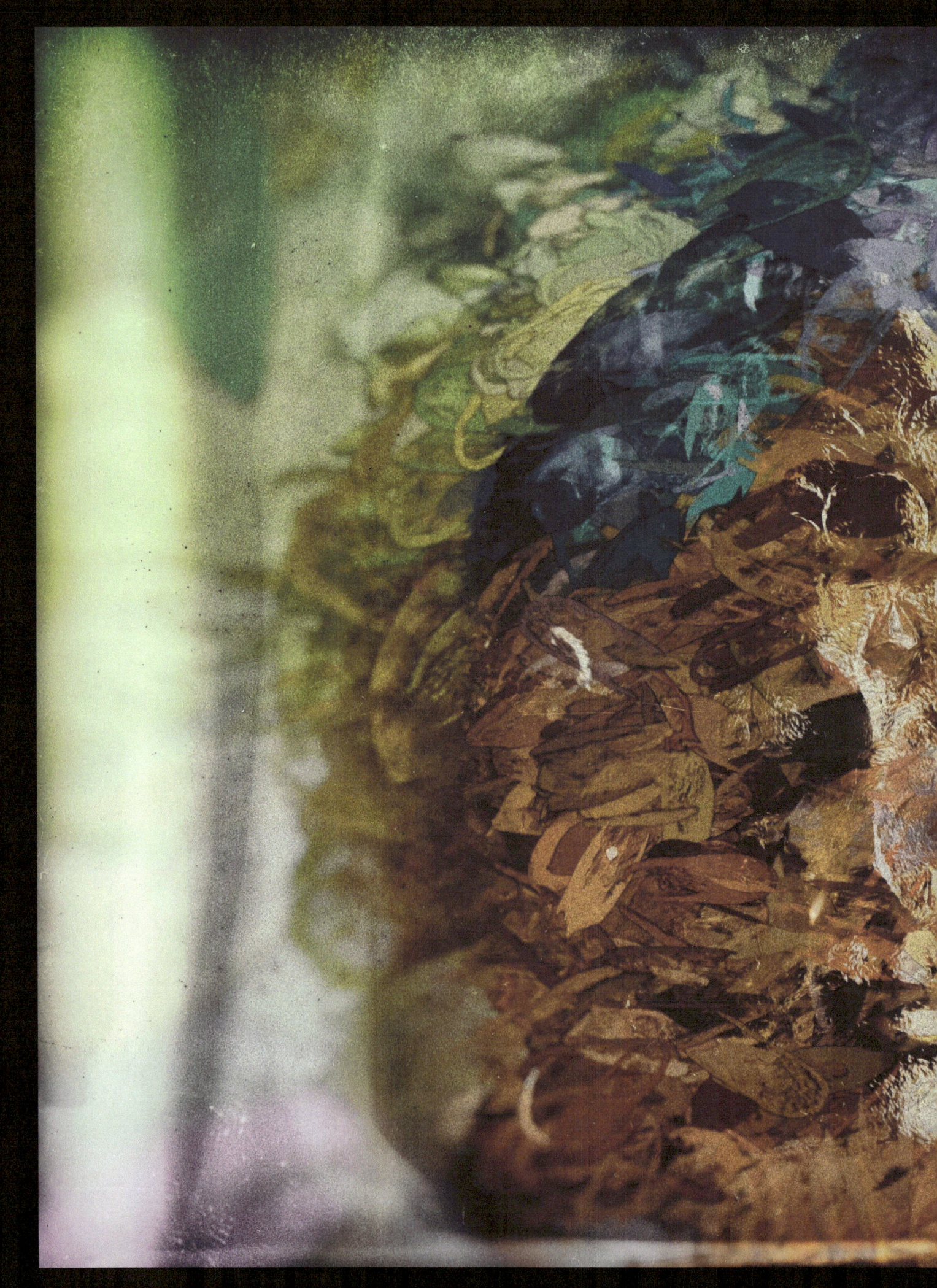

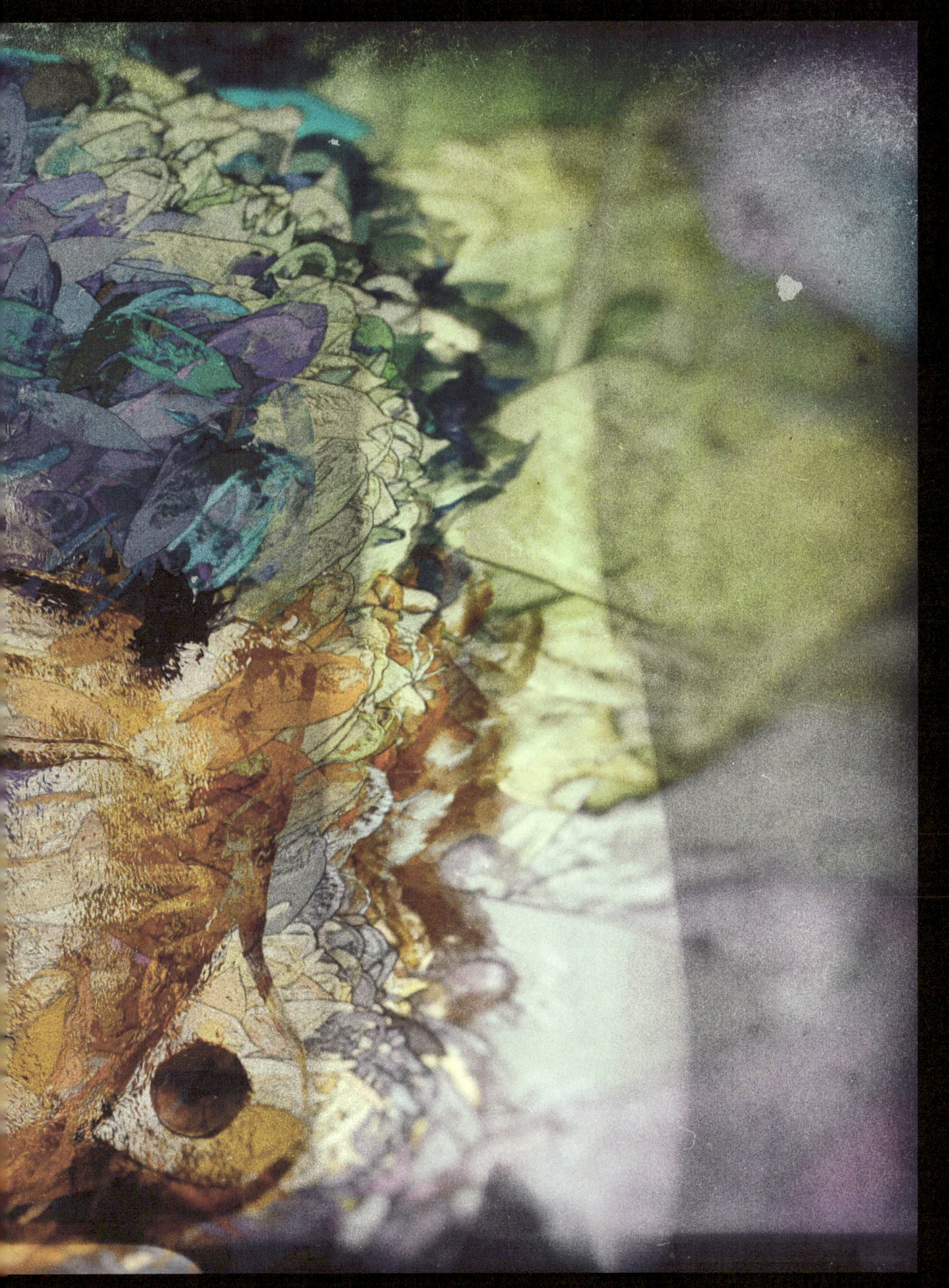

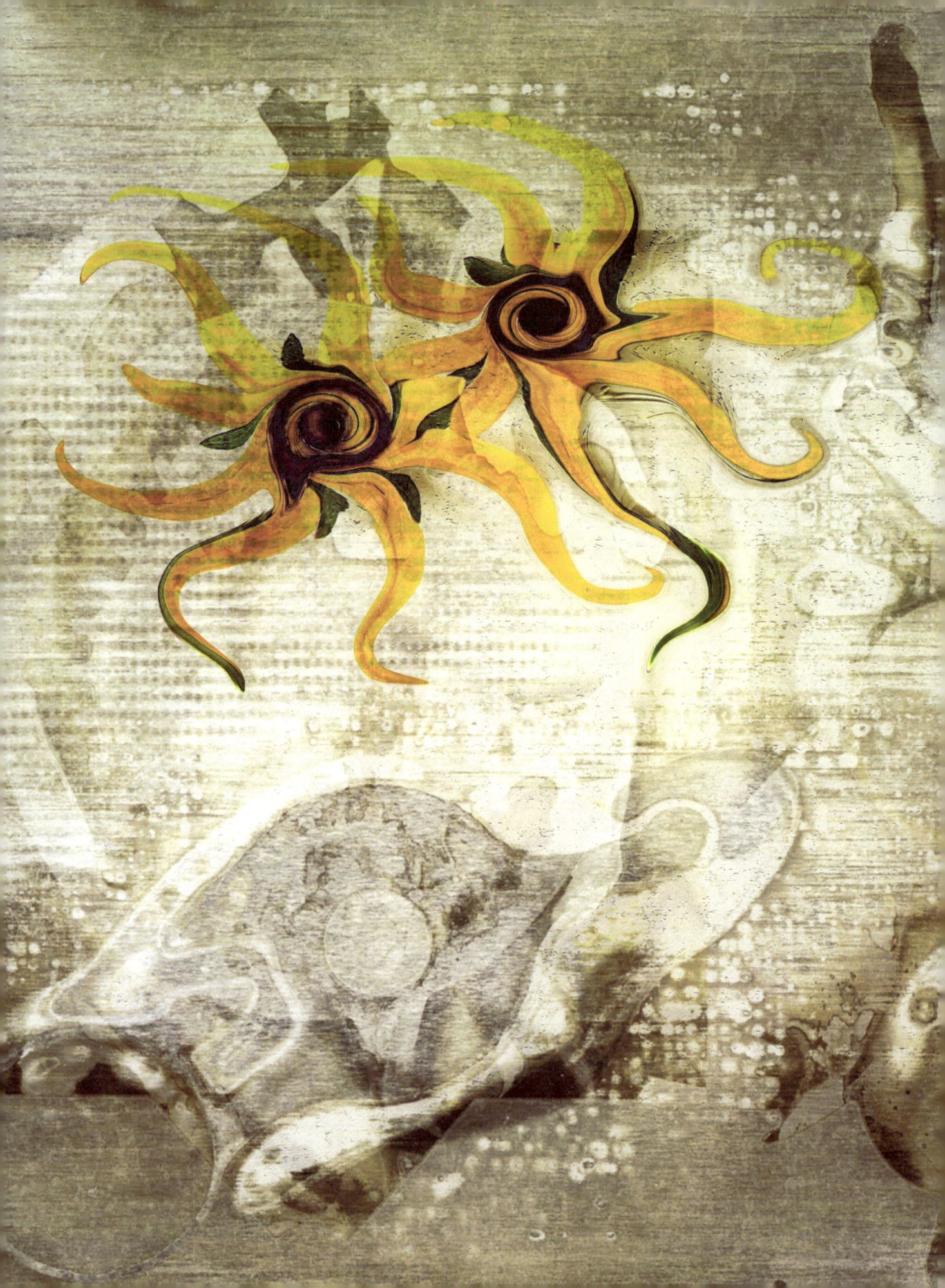

BNA Photography is a young company created by photographer Natacha Allard.

Established in Quebec, BNA Photography is specialized in photos art deco. His works are ideas for the homestaging, interior decoration ect.

BNA Photography creates for the moment two magazines per year, display his talent and his commercial works high style.

And this for all the bugets.

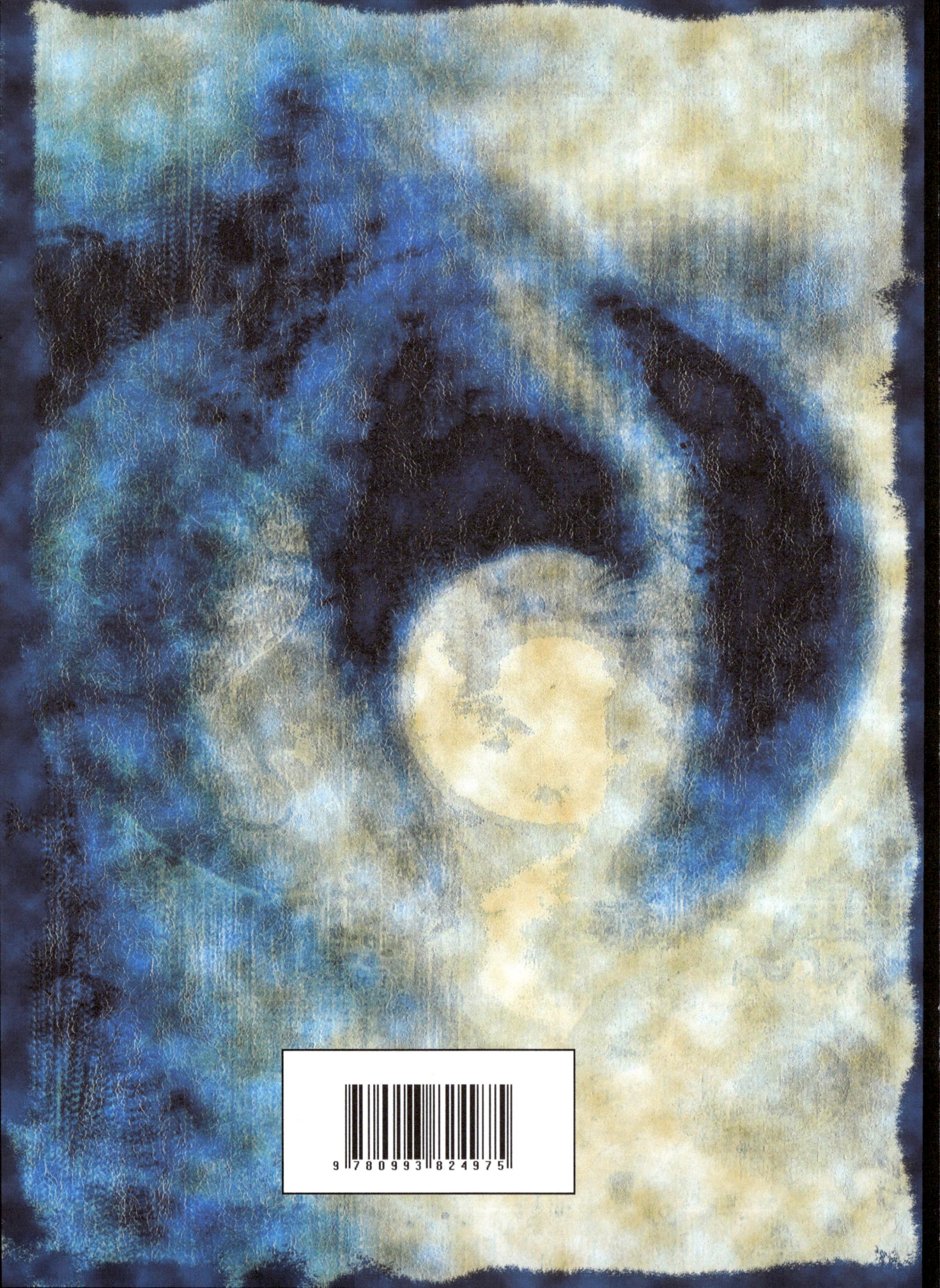

www.ingramcontent.com/pod-product-compliance
Lightning Source LLC
Chambersburg PA
CBHW040743200526
45159CB00023B/1654